KATE VENTER

MEREHURST PRESS
LONDON

© 1984 Tafelberg Publishers Ltd
This edition distributed in the U.K., E.E.C., Middle East,
Canada and U.S.A. by Merehurst Distribution
Ferry House, 51-57 Lacy Road, Putney, London SW15 1PR

Designed by G&G Design
Photography by Tony Abegglen
Illustrations by Janet Walker
Set in 10 on 12 Plantin by Diatype Setting
Colour separations by Unifoto
Printed and bound by Toppan Printing Co. (H.K.) Ltd,
Hong Kong
First edition 1984, seventh impression 1989

ISBN 0 948075 05 8

Contents

Basic equipment and aids

A collection of basic equipment (see plate 1) is an essential investment for the serious cake decorator.

You can build this up gradually as you progress in sugar art.

The icing bag

Bags made of material are on the market, but it is advisable to make your own out of greaseproof paper as these are easier to handle and more hygienic.

Cut out a rectangle of 230 mm x 350 mm from a piece of greaseproof paper (refer to first diagram on fig. 1). Fold over diagonally so that a and b on the second diagram are of equal length. Number the points as indicated on the third diagram. Lie flat with point 1 on your left and the short side running parallel to the table. Fold the paper over to the right and flatten to form point 4. Unfold again.

Press point 4 firmly onto the table with the right-hand thumb and turn point 1 in with the left hand as

Plate 1
Basic equipment for
sugar art

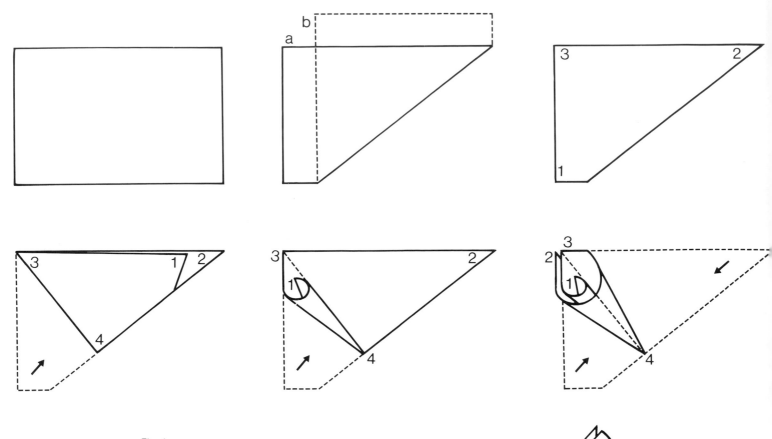

Fig. 1
How to fold the icing bag

indicated on the fifth diagram of fig. 1. Grip points 1 and 3 firmly.

Now fold point 2 over with the right hand from right to left around the front to bring it in line with point 3 at the back. Pull tight and grip firmly to form point 4. Pin 1, 3 and 2 together on the outside with a sterilised pin. Cut away point 4 to form an opening of 15 mm (see last diagram), or adjust this size to the corresponding icing pipe.

Insert the tube into the cut point, fill the bag with royal icing and fold up firmly by bringing the highest point at the back forward, folding the two sides inwards and then rolling up the top end to the front.

Icing tubes

For embroidery, writing and lace work, as well as for the formation of dots and lines, *writing tubes* in six different sizes are necessary. These are Nos 000, 00, 0, 1, 2 and 3.

Star tubes, which are serrated at the narow end, vary in numerical size according to make. With the Tala tube as basis for comparison, a set of three, Nos 5, 7 and 13, will be enough for the beginner.

For piping blossoms, little roses, lace, frills,

ribbons and so on, *petal* and *leaf tubes* are necessary. They are on the market, and like the star tubes, vary in numerical size according to make. Leaf tubes can be be substituted with homemade bags: fold a bag according to fig. 1 but only as far as the sixth diagram – do not cut away the sharp tip of the cone. Fill the bag with royal icing up to the tip. Fold the top end up as described in the last paragraph under *The icing bag*.

Flatten the tip (see first diagram of fig. 2), cut across (5 mm above the tip) and cut an inverted V about 2 mm deep in the middle of it. Make 3 mm diagonal cuts on either side of the legs of the V to form a W (see last diagram of fig. 2).

To form a leaf, place the point of the tube on a board. Press the bag and simultaneously lift the hand. Gradually decrease the pressure to let the leaf end in a sharp point. The greater the pressure the larger the leaf, and vice versa.

The W in the size given above is a good average to practise with. Work on a board at first and allow the piped leaves to dry and harden. You can work directly onto a cake at a later stage when you have acquired the necessary confidence. The size of the W can then also be adjusted accordingly.

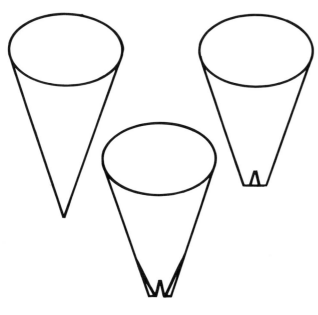

In order to form a very small leaf, follow a different procedure when cutting the bag. Do not make a horizontal cut above the tip, but two diagonal cuts of 3 mm each that will cross each other in the middle to form a V (see fig. 3).

Baking tins

Standard round or square cakes are baked in 30 cm, 20 cm and 15 cm tins. When you bake a fruit cake, line the tin or tins as follows:

Measure the circumference and the height of the tin, then, adding 2 cm for the length and 2 cm for the width, cut out two corresponding rectangles from brown paper and one from greaseproof paper. These are used to line the inside of the tin. Fold 2 cm back along one of the lengths and unfold again. Make cuts up to the crease all along this 2 cm strip. Grease the tin well and position the first piece of brown paper around the inside so that the fringed strip will lie on the bottom. Press the paper firmly against the side of the tin. Grease with butter or margarine then repeat the whole procedure with the second piece of brown and greaseproof paper.

Now cut two pieces of brown and one of greaseproof paper to fit the bottom of the tin. Line as for the sides.

Do *not* grease the last layer as the shortening in the recipe on p. 11 will prevent the cake from sticking to it.

Finally tie four layers of newspaper around the tin. This ensures that an even temperature will spread through the cake from the outside to the inside, which will result in a cake with a flat, not a rounded surface.

Turntable

This can be made of wood, as in plate 1, or of stainless steel. It is not essential, as a cake or biscuit tin can be used instead but it does make matters easier.

Modelling tools

Wooden or plastic tools are available in sets and are essential for modelling leaves, petals and miscellaneous figures. Pewter tools can be used instead if you like. Marzipan and plastic icing or flower paste are mainly used for modelling work.

Mixing bowls

Plastic bowls should not be used for mixing as they contain a certain amount of grease. Use earthenware, glass or stainless-steel bowls instead.

Knives

Three sets of knives will be enough for the beginner: a small spatula or spreader for mixing and spreading royal icing; a palette knife or artist's spatula with a blade of approximately 20 mm x 110 mm for lifting and handling small petals, leaves, lace work, figures and so on, and a scalpel for cutting out designs and making small or fine cuts.

Brushes

Approximately five round artist's brushes (Nos 00, 0, 1, 2 and 3) are necessary for flood work and for painting flowers and other motifs. A No. 6 round brush for dusting flowers with chalk is also recommended. Invest in two flat-tipped brushes (Nos 10 and 1 respectively) for rice-paper painting.

Chalk

Edible chalk is used in dry form to colour and give depth to designs and flowers. A wide variety of tints and shades can be obtained by mixing white and the three basic colours (red, blue and yellow). Colours can be lightened with cornstarch instead of white chalk. A wide range of commercial colours are also available.

Rulers

In addition to an ordinary ruler a handy set of four circular dividers are available for marking cakes into various sections.

Rose nails

This consists of a metal nail for easy handling and a flat top of approximately 2,5 cm to 3 cm in diameter to serve as a base on which to make flowers from royal icing. A practical rose nail can be made by using a bottle top stuck onto the head of a long and fairly thin nail.

Florist's tape

A self-adhesive tape is available in different colours. A special cutter, as shown in plate 1, is a very useful device for cutting the tape into even halves, thirds or quarters. Green tape is used for covering florist's wire to make stems for flowers, leaves and so on.

Florist's ribbon, available in standard widths, is used together with flowers for a more delicate look in

Fig. 2
How to cut the icing
bag to replace the leaf
tube

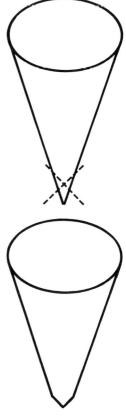

Fig. 3
How to cut the icing
bag to pipe very small
leaves

arrangements. It can also be divided with a tape cutter.

Wire-cutter
This should be very sharp and of good quality so that the wire stems of flowers can be cut neatly into required lengths.

Cutters
These are used for pressing out shapes such as keys, numbers, letters, petals, leaves and other figures of flower paste or plastic icing.

Work board
This serves as a general work surface. I find that a 25 cm x 30 cm board is a useful size and prefer a wooden board covered with self-adhesive plastic in a pastel chequered design.

Tweezers
These are indispensable for delicate work. A standard pair and a long pair with a curved point should form part of your basic equipment.

Stamens
These can be found in different colours in hobby and craft shops. White and yellow are mainly used, and the finer they are, the more delicate the work. You can also manage quite well with white only if you use colouring to dye this for your requirements.

Pastry cutters
Three kinds are necessary: a pastry cutter for cutting designs out of plastic icing or flower paste; a dressmaker's tracing wheel to copy a design onto a cake and to finish off paste ribbons, imitate stitching and so on; and a parsley cutter for cutting plastic icing or flower paste into even strips for ribbons.

Florist's wire
This is obtainable in different gauges and is used mainly for flower stems. I usually keep Nos 18, 20, 22, 24 and 26 in stock.

Scissors
Two pairs are necessary: an ordinary pair for cutting out paper patterns and a small pair with long, sharp blades for making flowers out of flower paste.

Rolling-pins
Different sizes are used for rolling out marzipan, plastic icing and flower paste. A small one for flower paste can be made out of a piece of chrome tubing or towel rail (approximately 18 mm in diameter and 150 mm in length).

Muslin cloth
Cover royal icing with a damp muslin cloth to prevent it from forming a crust. Strain the white of an egg through a piece of dry cloth to prevent threads of egg white breaking up in the icing. Shape a piece of dry cloth into a pad and use it to smooth marzipan or plastic icing.

Colouring
Vegetable colouring is available in liquid, powder and paste form, all of which are used for the same purpose.

Gum powder
Mix gum powder into plastic icing to make flower paste with a more pliable consistency. Two kinds are available: gum tragacanth which is very expensive, and carboxy methyl cellulose or CMC which also results in a whiter flower paste.

Polystyrene
The stems of completed flowers may be stuck into blocks of polystyrene for drying and storage, and modelled petals or leaves can be placed in individual cups of polystyrene fruit containers for shaping and drying.

Table tennis balls or marbles
These are used for drying shaped petals and other rounded designs (see plate 6).

Sugar thermometer
Essential for preparing plastic icing and making rocks from sugar (see p. 32).

Recipes

Firm cakes such as fruit cakes and madeira cakes, which can be covered with marzipan and fondant are mainly used for the delicate art of cake decorating as they keep for a long time. Sponge and butter cakes are too light for this method. The following recipe has been used for the past 25 years or more and is most reliable. For those who would like a rich light fruit cake I provide an alternative recipe.

Rich fruit cake

400 g raisins
400 g currants
400 g sultanas
400 g cherries
60 g glacé ginger, chopped
60 g fig preserve, chopped
60 g watermelon preserve, chopped
60 g glacé pineapple, chopped
275 g dates, chopped
175 g mixed peel
125 ml brandy
450 g cake flour
2 ml salt
10 ml ground cinnamon
10 ml ground mixed spice
5 ml ground nutmeg
5 ml ground ginger
5 ml baking powder
2 ml mace
2 ml ground cloves
350 g butter
350 g yellow sugar
8 eggs
2,5 ml bicarbonate of soda, dissolved in 15 ml strong black coffee
15 ml vanilla essence
8 ml almond essence
125 ml Van der Hum

Wash raisins, currants, sultanas and cherries thoroughly and leave to dry. If the rest of the fruit is very syrupy or sugary, wash and dry thoroughly as well. Mix all the fruit together in a large mixing bowl, and pour over the brandy.

Line the pans with two layers of brown and one layer of greaseproof paper, and tie a few layers of newspaper around the outside. (Refer to the instructions on p. 9.) Sift all the dry ingredients, except the bicarbonate of soda.

Cream butter and sugar, and beat three eggs in one by one. Fold in a little of the sifted dry ingredients after the third egg.

Sprinkle two handsful of dry ingredients over the fruit mixture and mix well.

Mix the rest of the dry ingredients and the remaining five eggs alternately into the butter mixture. Mix well. Add the bicarbonate of soda dissolved in the coffee, as well as the two flavourings. Mix well. Add to the fruit and mix thoroughly.

Spoon into the prepared tins and bake for approximately 3½ hours as follows: 1 hour at 180 °C (350 °F), 1 hour at 150 °C (300 °F), 1 hour at 130 °C (250 °F) and 30 minutes at 100 °C (200 °F).

An alternative baking method is to bake overnight. First bake the cake for 30 minutes at 150 °C (300 °F), then for 30 minutes at 130 °C (250 °F), then for approximately six hours at 100 °C (200 °F). The full baking time, therefore, is approximately seven hours.

Remove from the oven and pour the Van der Hum over the cakes; then allow to cool in the tins.

This mixture yields one round cake of 250 mm in diameter or two round cakes of 200 mm in diameter or one square cake of 230 mm x 230 mm.

For a round cake of 300 mm in diameter use 1½ times the ingredients; for a square cake of 300 mm x 300 mm use twice the ingredients; for a round cake of 350 mm in diameter use twice the ingredients; for a square cake of 350 mm x 350 mm use 2½ times the ingredients; for two round cakes of respectively 250 mm and 150 mm in diameter, use 1¼ times the ingredients; and for two square cakes of 230 mm x 230 mm and 150 mm x 150 mm respectively use 1¼ times the ingredients.

Light fruit cake

450 g whole cherries, washed and dried
350 g sultanas *or* 225 g sultanas and 125 g ginger preserve
125 g mixed peel
225 g fig preserve, washed, dried and chopped
225 g pineapple rings, drained, washed and chopped
225 g ground almonds
handful whole almonds
450 g cake flour
275 g butter
225 g sugar
10 ml baking powder
pinch salt

5 large or 6 small eggs
10 ml almond essence
80 ml to 125 ml cherry or peach liqueur

Mix the fruit and nuts in a large mixing bowl. Sprinkle a handful of flour over the fruit and mix in well.

Line a cake tin of 250 mm in diameter as described on p. 9.

Cream the butter and sugar.

Sift the flour, baking powder and salt together.

Add the eggs singly to the butter mixture, beating well after each addition. Add the flour mixture gradually, then the flavouring and fruit, and mix well.

Bake for 3 to 3½ hours at 140 to 150 °C (275 to 300 °F) until done.

Remove from the oven and pour over the liqueur immediately.

Allow to cool in tins.

Balance in tiered cakes
Good proportions for a three tiered cake are round tins with a diameter of 300 mm, 200 mm and 150 mm respectively, or 350 mm, 250 mm and 180 mm. Dimensions of square cakes must be in the same proportion. The diameter of the cake drums for the largest cake should be approximately 400 mm, then 250 mm and 190 mm for the two smaller cakes.

Fig. 4
How to obtain balance for a tiered cake

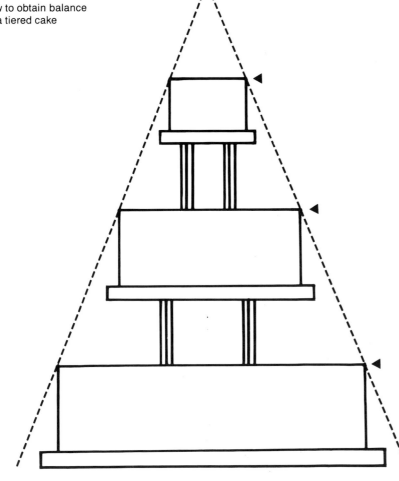

When the cakes are arranged on dividers on top of each other a ruler positioned against the side of all three cakes should touch the upper edge of each cake (see arrows on fig. 4).

There must also be a difference of at least 12 mm in the height of the three cakes, with the highest layer at the bottom. So if the largest cake, which will carry the heaviest decorations, is approximately 90 mm high, the middle cake should be 78 mm and the top one 66 mm.

Butter icing
125 g butter or margarine
500 g icing sugar
any liquid – water, milk, cream or fruit juice
5 ml flavouring
pinch salt
colouring (optional)

Beat the butter, add the icing sugar gradually, beating well after each addition, until creamy. If the mixture is too thick, add enough warm liquid to obtain a soft and creamy mixture. Cold liquid will cause the mixture to curdle.

Add the flavouring and salt when well mixed. Colour if desired.

Add the white or the yolk of an egg for a richer and less creamy consistency, but use 30 g less butter.

Glacé icing and marbling
Glacé icing is cheap and can be made in minutes. The only two ingredients are icing sugar and any liquid at room temperature: water, orange juice or any other fruit juice. Colour if necessary.

Combine icing sugar and liquid and mix quickly to form a consistency that will spread over the cake without running off it. Work quickly as a crust forms rapidly.

You can't make decorations with this icing, but by colouring part of it with chocolate, for example, a marble effect can be obtained. Spread the plain colour evenly over the top of the cake and then pipe lines over it in the second colour with a No. 2 writing tube.

Use a knitting-needle or similar tool and draw cross-lines about 15 mm apart in the second colour. Work to and fro in a flowing movement, first from right to left and then from left to right.

The second colour can also be piped onto the cake in a spiral, with the circles about 25 mm apart. Once again use a knitting-needle or similar tool and draw alternate lines in a flowing movement across the spiral lines from the centre to the edge and from the edge to the centre around the top of the cake.

Work as quickly as possible so that the lines are drawn before the icing sets.

A marble effect can also be obtained with butter icing: cover the cake with ordinary butter icing and then soften a small quantity of prepared icing with liquid so that the thinned down icing will flood easily over the first layer. You can then follow the same methods as for glacé icing.

Almond paste or marzipan

Almond paste can be obtained commercially in large quantities. Although this is not pure almond paste, it is a very good substitute for the real thing (see recipe below). For a more economical mixture, the yolk or white of an egg, or a whole egg, can be added to the almond paste together with enough icing sugar to obtain a workable consistency. A little cherry liqueur, brandy, ratafia essence or vanilla essence to taste can be added to improve the flavour.

Never roll the marzipan out on cornstarch as this has a tendency to ferment and can totally spoil a beautiful piece of work. Always roll out on icing sugar.

Uncooked almond paste

500 g ground almonds
250 g icing sugar
250 g castor sugar
10 ml brandy or cherry liqueur
± 8 egg yolks, beaten

Mix all dry ingredients together; then add brandy or liqueur. Add enough egg yolk to form a firm paste. Knead until just mixed. Too much kneading will make the paste very greasy.

Cooked almond paste

450 g granulated sugar
130 ml water
10 ml liquid glucose (light corn syrup can also be used)
350 g ground almonds
2 egg whites, unbeaten
2 ml almond essence
2 ml ratafia essence
2 ml vanilla essence
5 ml lemon juice

Pour the sugar and water into the top of a double boiler and place directly on the stove with the lid on. Heat over a low temperature until dissolved.

Add the glucose, and boil to a temperature of 115 °C (220 °F). Take off the stove, pour hot water into the bottom section of the double boiler, and replace the top. The bottom of the upper section must not touch the water. Add the almonds and egg whites and mix well.

Replace on the stove and boil slowly for 3 to 5 minutes, stirring continuously.

Pour out onto a well-greased marble slab or into a shallow flat enamel dish.

Pour the flavourings over the paste and paddle with a wooden spoon or a broad metal spatula until well mixed and firm.

How to cover a cake with almond paste

Spread a very thin layer of apricot jam over the entire cake to ensure that the almond paste will stick to the surface. Do not use too much jam as the icing sugar that adheres to the almond paste will melt. The resulting syrup will leak through the base of the cake, especially if it is very moist.

Use enough almond paste to form a roll of approximately 50 mm to 60 mm in diameter and 450 mm long. Press flat with the palm of the hand then roll out widthwise and lengthwise with a rolling pin to form a rectangle that corresponds with the height and circumference of the cake. Cut straight.

Sift a small amount of icing sugar over the paste and roll up as for a Swiss roll. Place the free end of the roll against the side of the cake, press firmly against the side with the left hand and unroll around the cake with the right hand. (The side that was sprinkled with icing sugar will now be on the outside.)

Press the paste firmly onto the cake and smooth with the palm of the hand. Never press the fingers against the paste as this will leave marks.

Make a pad with a piece of dry muslin cloth, and smooth and polish the cake all over.

Roll out enough paste to cover the top of the cake. Lift carefully onto the cake and roll lightly with a rolling pin. Cut the excess paste away with a pair of scissors so that the top and bottom meet neatly. Rub the palm of the hand over the join until well sealed and almost invisible. Finish off by rubbing with the muslin pad.

Uncooked fondant or plastic icing

10 ml gelatine
50 ml cold water
250 g liquid glucose
1 egg white
1 kg icing sugar
20 g white vegetable fat

Soak the gelatine in the cold water and place over hot water until dissolved and clear. Do not boil as it will become sticky. Melt the glucose in the same way.

Mix the egg white, gelatine and glucose. Gradually stir in the icing sugar, reserving 250 ml. Mix slowly but thoroughly.

Sift the remaining 250 ml of icing sugar onto a clean and dry work surface. Pour the egg white/gelatine/glucose/sugar mixture onto this. Knead enough of this dry icing sugar into the paste to form a soft, workable consistency, while adding the white vegetable fat gradually. If the mixture is too stiff, add extra egg white or a small amount of water. If too soft, mix in more icing sugar.

Cooked fondant or plastic icing

10 ml gelatine
25 ml cold water
225 g white granulated sugar

225 g liquid glucose
125 ml hot water
3 to 4 x 500 g packets of white icing sugar
30 g white vegetable fat

Soak the gelatine in the cold water and keep aside.

Melt the water, sugar and glucose in an enamel or stainless-steel pot. Never use aluminium pots for this purpose as this will discolour the mixture. Brush the sides of the pot with water and put the lid on to dissolve all the sugar granules that might have stuck to the sides. Remove the lid as soon as steam starts escaping.

Put a sugar thermometer into the syrup and boil until a temperature of 106 °C (220 °F) is reached. Remove from the stove and add gelatine immediately. Stir until completely dissolved. Undissolved gelatine will cause unsightly dark specks in the icing. Leave for a while until all the bubbles have come to the surface.

Sift and add enough icing sugar gradually to the mixture until it becomes too difficult to stir. Do not stir too much as too many air bubbles will form in the paste.

Cover a clean, dry work surface well with sifted icing sugar, and pour the mixture onto this. Knead in the fat, and enough icing sugar to form a workable paste. The correct amount of icing sugar will determine the success of the icing. If too soft it will slide off the cake; if too stiff it will form a dry, cracked and unsightly covering.

Roll out the icing on dry icing sugar until about 8 mm thick. Remember not to use maize flour or cornstarch. The size and shape of the rolled fondant must correspond with that of the cake.

Brush the almond paste on the cake with egg white or a little water. Take care not to make the surface too wet, or the fondant will slide off the cake.

Push hands palm-down far enough under the rolled out fondant to lift it up completely on the backs of the hands and forearms and place carefully over the cake. The cake should be on the table and not the turntable at this stage to prevent the weight of the overhanging sides of the fondant from cracking and tearing.

Roll over the top with a rolling pin and press the sides firmly with the palms of the hands. Do not leave finger prints! Trim the excess icing around the bottom edge of the cake and rub the fondant with a muslin pad until smooth and glossy.

Excess fondant can be stored in a plastic bag in an airtight container at room temperature for later use.

Royal icing

This is made with egg white and sifted icing sugar and is mainly used for making tube flowers, flood work, and finishing off the sides of cakes with embroidery, lace work and filigree.

1 egg white, at room temperature
± 200 g icing sugar

Strain the egg white through a dry muslin cloth. This will break up the egg white yet retain the thickening. Beat lightly.

Sift the icing sugar through a very fine sieve, nylon stocking, a piece of organdy or something similar. Add gradually to the egg white and mix to form a soft, creamy consistency. Add just enough icing sugar so that when the spoon is lifted out of the mixture a sharp and smooth peak forms and holds. If the icing mixture is too soft, the peak will curl back. If too much icing sugar has been used the peak will break off bluntly.

If too stiff, dip a spatula with a small quantity of icing mixture on it, into beaten egg white and mix this into the rest of the icing mixture. Repeat this process until the correct consistency is reached. This method will prevent you from ending up with an enormous bowl of mixed icing.

Royal icing will be snow white if it has been mixed correctly. To make it even brighter, dip the tip of the handle of a brush into blue colouring and mix this trace into the icing. If not well mixed, it will be slightly cream in colour.

Flood icing

Flood icing has a runny consistency but is not as liquid as water. The first step is to mix a quantity of royal icing (described above). Cover with a damp muslin cloth.

The next step is to thin down small quantities of royal icing with cold water or egg white to flood a pattern in relief. (For examples of this type of work see plates 10 to 14.) It is not possible to give exact proportions of the ingredients as the individual pieces of a design filled with different colours of flood icing will differ in size and shape. However, there is a test to determine approximately how much icing should be thinned for a specific area.

Use a small quantity of mixed royal icing and thin down in a separate bowl. Draw a line through the icing with the sharp edge of a knife. The consistency will be correct if the line does not close up before the count of seven. This measure is used in warm, dry weather. In cold and/or wet conditions the mixture can be slightly thicker and a count of 10 is used for the test.

To work out how much flood icing to colour for a specific area of a pattern, pour a spoonful of the mixture onto a wax-covered board. Leave to spread and set. You can then work out how many spoonfuls to prepare. Remember that it is better to mix a little more than you need, as it is virtually impossible to repeat a tint or shade.

Trace the pattern for a specific cake onto grease-proof paper down to the finest detail. Never use the original pattern to work on as parts of the design will be covered with flood icing as work begins which will make it necessary to refer to the original design.

After tracing the pattern, place it on a flat surface like a piece of glass, wooden board or cake drum, and secure with either Sellotape or drawing pins. The work board should be light and easy to handle.

Subsequently place a sheet of wax paper over the greaseproof paper and secure carefully. If the design moves during the flooding process the surface will crack and look unsightly. An alternative method is to place the greaseproof paper with the design underneath a sheet of glass and secure firmly. Wash or clean, and spread the top of the glass with a small amount of vegetable fat before you begin to work.

Study the pattern intensively. In case certain sections can be flooded separately for a three-dimensional effect, such as the arm from the side view of the little fisherman (see plate 13), trace and place under wax paper on a separate board or under glass.

Decide which sections on the picture are furthest in perspective from the viewer, and mark No. 1. Number each individual section from No. 2 upwards moving towards the viewer. When the flood work begins, the picture is built up in dimensions by working gradually from the back to the front, that is, starting with No. 1 and ending with the highest number.

The next step is to colour enough royal icing in separate bowls for the different sections of the picture. Please note that best results for dark colours are obtained by using dry undiluted powdered colouring.

Divide each colour between two bowls. The one quantity remains as it is, while the other is thinned down as described for flood work. Never work the other way around (first colouring the flood icing then thickening it for the piping) as this will result in the icing for the outline being lighter than the icing for the flood work.

Start with section 1. Outline with a No. 1 writing tube and the appropriate colour in royal icing, then flood the space carefully with the corresponding colour in flood icing. (An icing bag without a tube can be used for this purpose – cut the opening to the size of a No. 1 tube.) Under no circumstances must the picture be outlined all at once as this will spoil the three-dimensional effect that you want to achieve. Do not fill the outlines with too much flood icing either as it will flow onto other sections of the pattern.

Pipe flood icing into the centre of the outlined section and work this gradually up to the edges with a No. 1 round-tipped paintbrush of good quality. Paint the flood icing carefully onto the outline so that an integrated whole will be formed without the icing overflowing onto the wax paper.

Flood the rest of the picture in a similar fashion, according to the numbers. In case No. 2, for example, should be next to section No. 1, the latter should be left

until completely dry before beginning the former.

Some sections will obviously overlap other sections, like a hand on material or a bow in the hair. If this is the case, great care must be taken not to disturb the perspective. For instance, fingers can look like bananas if made too large. If the hand rests on clothing, the clothing should be flooded first. Pipe the outline of the clothing with royal icing, just inside the outlines of the hand. When this has been flooded the outline of the hand, corresponding exactly in size to the pattern, will be piped on top of the edge of the clothing, and then filled with flood icing to normal size. The hand will then automatically be higher than the clothing.

The swan in plate 10 is a good pattern for the beginner to use for developing skills and acquiring experience.

Modelling paste
This paste is used for making flowers and assorted free-standing figures.

Uncooked modelling paste
This recipe is mostly used during the summer months.

± 500 g plastic icing
15 ml gum tragacanth or CMC (see p. 10)
± 10 ml egg white
± 30 g white vegetable fat

Mix the gum into the plastic icing and knead well. The gum must be thoroughly incorporated into the paste before the egg white is added. Add the egg white, knead in the vegetable fat and knead until the paste is smooth and elastic.

Put in a plastic bag and place in an airtight container. Allow to rest for 24 hours before using. Do not store in refrigerator.

Knead the paste very well and add more egg white if necessary.

With the correct treatment and handling this paste can keep for months. Store in a plastic bag in an airtight container in a cool place and knead well every second or third day.

Cooked modelling paste
Mainly for use during the wet, cold winter months.

450 g icing sugar, sifted
15 ml gum tragacanth or CMC (see p. 10)
10 ml gelatine, soaked in 25 ml cold water
45 ml egg white
60 g white vegetable fat

Grease a large mixing bowl with vegetable fat and place on top of a pot of hot water. The bottom of the bowl should not touch the water.

Sift half the icing sugar together with the gum

tragacanth into the mixing bowl. Place the pot on the stove and bring the water to the boil to warm the icing sugar. Pour the rest of the icing sugar into a second mixing bowl and warm in the oven which must be set on a low temperature. The icing sugar must not get too hot as this will destroy the elasticity of the gelatine when it is added.

In the meantime place the soaked gelatine in a small container over hot water to dissolve and clarify. Do not boil.

Remove the pot cum mixing bowl from the stove and make a well in the centre of the icing mixture. Pour the egg white and dissolved gelatine into this, and stir in the sifted sugar mixture gradually. Beat very well until white and creamy.

Remove icing sugar from the oven and add it gradually to the mixture to make a smooth and pliable paste. Grease the surface of the work board with a little of the fat and knead the paste on it. Add small pieces of the rest of the fat gradually to the paste and knead until smooth, elastic and cold.

Put in a plastic bag in an airtight container and leave to rest for 24 hours before use. For storage, see the last paragraph under *Uncooked modelling paste*.

How to colour modelling paste

Use as much paste as will be necessary to complete all the flowers or figures that will be made from a particular colour. Remember that it is better to prepare a little more than you might need as it is virtually impossible to repeat shades and tints.

Divide the prepared white paste into two equal portions. Colour the one portion in the darkest tint that will be required and keep the other portion aside in a plastic bag.

Divide the coloured paste in two, with one portion slightly larger than the other. Put the larger portion in a plastic bag in an airtight container (call this A).

Divide the second portion of white paste in two. Put one half in a plastic bag and mix the other half with the smaller portion of the coloured paste. Knead well then divide this lighter tint in two, again making one portion larger than the other. Keep the larger portion (call this tint B) in a plastic bag in an airtight container, and mix the smaller portion with the balance of the white paste for an even lighter tint (C). (See fig. 5.)

It is also possible to alter the contrast between the three tints by adding more white paste as desired.

Fig. 5
How to mix modelling paste to obtain three tints of the same colour

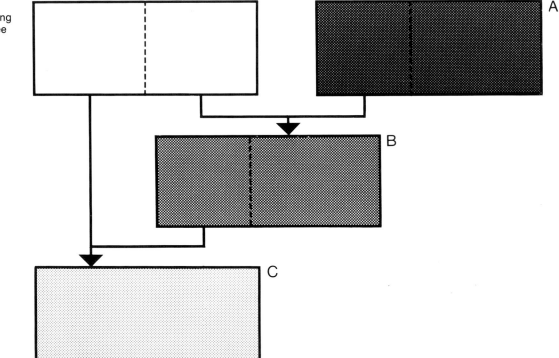

Icing methods and techniques

Royal icing flowers

Forget-me-nots

Cover a work board or cake drum with wax paper. Colour the icing bright blue, put in a piping bag with a No. 1 writing tube and pipe five dots (representing the flower petals) close together on the paper to form a circle.

First pipe a small dot at the top to represent the first petal, then pipe two dots slightly lower down on either side of it. Pipe another two dots directly under these to complete the circle. Finally, pipe a small yellow dot with a No. 1 writing tube in the centre (see plate 2).

When completely dry these can be attached to a small piece of wire for use in flower arrangements. They can also be used on the sides of cakes as part of embroidery work or piped directly onto the cake.

Rosebuds

These pretty little rosebuds (approximately 10 mm in diameter) are very useful to use in embroidery patterns on a cake.

Put a small amount of royal icing on a rose nail and attach a square piece of wax paper (see plate 2). Use a No. 73 or 74 Errington tube and the desired colour of royal icing. Place the wide end of the tube on the wax paper on the nail, with the indentation towards you. Don't hold the tube too firmly against the rose nail as it will be impossible to turn the nail.

Hold the tube in an upright position. Press the piping bag with the right hand while you turn the rose nail in the left hand in an anti-clockwise direction to form a spiral (the centre of the flower). This spiral must be pointed at the top.

Turn the rose nail so that the end of the spiral will be in the ten-o'clock position. Place the wide end of the tube in the twelve-o'clock position at the base of the spiral, with the narrow end slightly towards the outside and the tube at an angle of approximately 45°. Press the bag and turn the rose nail anti-clockwise, but form only a half circle. Lift off.

Place the tube against the base of the petal in the same way to overlap it by approximately one-third. Turn the rose nail while you press the bag to form another half circle.

Leave to dry thoroughly. Hold the rose bud in your left hand, with the flat side towards you. Pipe five dots in green royal icing in a No. 2 tube around the base. Place the tube in the centre of these dots, and press the bag for a few seconds to form the hip. Continue squeezing while you move your hand away gradually to form the stem. Place on its side on a piece of wax paper to dry.

To make a larger rose of approximately 30 mm in diameter (see plate 2), make a cone with a No. 7 or 8 star tube (with wax paper on a rose nail). Leave to dry. Pipe a little spiral around the upper tip of the cone with a No. 71 or 69 Errington tube, then pipe three semi-circular petals around it as described for the rosebud. Form five similar petals lower down, and leave to dry. This is now ready for use (it is not necessary to make a calyx and stem).

These roses can be made in butter icing as well.

Blossoms

Very small blossoms made with a No. 73 or 74 Errington tube can be used effectively in embroidery. Use a No. 71 or 72 Errington tube or No. 42 Tala tube, if you have one, to make larger blossoms. (Unfortunately the Tala tube is no longer available on the market.)

Place a small piece of wax paper with royal icing on a rose nail. Position the wide end of the petal tube on the nail, with the indentation towards you. Hold the tube at an angle of 45° to ensure that the petals will not be too thick or curl too much.

Turn the nail in an anti-clockwise direction in your left hand while you squeeze the bag. Do not move your right hand. As soon as the petal has been formed, stop squeezing and lift the tube off.

Put the wide end of the tube slightly underneath the first petal and repeat the last procedure. Form three more petals in the same way so that there will be five petals overlapping each other in a circle (see plate 2).

Allow to dry. Push the one end of a No. 26 florist's wire through the middle of the flower. Pipe a small amount of green royal icing into the centre and press in yellow nonpareils to form stamens, or use artificial stamens that vary in length. The base of the petals can be painted with a darker colour for effect before the stamens are inserted. Paint the tips of the stamens with colouring.

Green royal icing can be substituted for florist's wire to form the stem (see instructions under rosebuds).

Plate 2
How to make forget-
me-nots, rose buds,
larger roses, blossoms,
small daisies and
larger daisies of royal
icing

finger tip and draw a line with a pin for the vein. Leave to dry.

Pipe a small quantity of royal icing in the same colour as the petals onto a square of wax paper. Insert the petals to form a circle. Support these with two semi-circles of sponge or foam rubber (the thicker the sponge and the smaller the hole in the centre the more closed the flower will be).

Make a hole in the centre while the icing is still soft to allow a wire stem to be inserted later on. Leave to dry.

Form a hook at the top end of a No. 24 florist's wire and bend over so that it will rest flat on the flower. Lift the flower carefully and push the wire stem through the hole. Cover the loop with yellow royal icing, taking care that a small amount of icing is underneath the hook. Pour nonpareils over the centre and shake off the excess. Leave to dry.

Modelling paste flowers

Specific measurements and colours are mentioned in the following instructions. The intention is not to prescribe, but to give an indication of the proportions between the different components, as the size and colour of the flowers are to correspond with the colour scheme and arrangements on the cake.

Anonymous flower

Roll a small piece of modelling paste into a teardrop. Press the bottom half flat to form a Mexican hat shape. Place a five-petal blossom cutter of approximately 15 mm in diameter over the "hat" and cut out. Lie on the palm of the hand with the point upwards and roll each petal with a ball modelling tool until very thin and slightly hollow.

Take the point of the flower in the left hand and press a little star into the trumpet with a fluted modelling tool (see plate 3). Draw the veins on the petals from the centre to the tip of each petal with a dressmaker's pin and make a hole through the trumpet. Tape three stamens of varying lengths to the top end of a piece of No. 26 florist's wire and push this through the trumpet.

Press the paste securely onto the stem and pinch each petal slightly to curl them backwards. Paint the tips of the stamens pink.

These flowers can be used individually, or taped together in a spray.

Blossoms

Colour the modelling paste as desired and roll very thinly. Cut out a shape using the same cutter as for the anonymous flower. Roll each petal very thinly with a ball tool and mark the divisions between each petal with a hat pin or dressmaker's pin. Press a small hole in the centre and insert a stamen which will serve as the stem. Secure with royal icing or egg white.

Small daisy (approximately 20 mm in diameter)
Use a No. 1 writing tube to form the petals, again using the rose nail and a piece of wax paper.

Form a series of "teardrops" with the wide end towards the outside and the pointed tips towards the inside (the tips must touch). First of all pipe two tears opposite each other and then two in between to form a cross. Fill the spaces between the legs of the cross with matching drops to form a circle of eight petals.

Allow to dry slightly, then press the petals with the tip of the finger to flatten them (see plate 2). Prick a hole in the centre of the flower that is big enough for the insertion of a No. 26 florist's wire. Allow to dry completely. Bend the top end of the wire into a hook, then bend the hook over into a horizontal position.

Pipe a small amount of green royal icing into the centre of the flower, insert the wire and pull the hook into the icing. Dip into yellow nonpareils and leave to dry thoroughly.

Paint the centre of the flower with a little colouring around the stamens and also highlight some of the tips of the stamens.

Larger daisies (approximately 35 mm in diameter)
These flowers (see plate 2) are made of individually piped petals which are assembled afterwards with royal icing.

Draw two parallel lines, approximately 20 mm apart, on a piece of greaseproof paper. Draw a few more pairs of lines directly underneath, with spaces in between. Secure the pattern on a wooden board and cover with wax paper as described earlier on.

Pipe tear drops between the lines with a No. 2 writing tube as for the small daisy. Flatten with the

18

Paint the centre of the flower with colouring and leave to dry thoroughly. Now make a few buds as follows (see plate 3):

Roll a small amount of modelling paste into a ball. Flatten and press the head of a stamen onto this with egg white. Roll between the fingers to form a small teardrop, about the same length as the radius of the flower. Leave to dry.

Tape the buds and flowers into sprays of your choice onto No. 26 florist's wire as described on p. 24 under *Cymbidium*.

Apple blossom

Form a small piece of modelling paste into a Mexican hat shape. Cut out the calyx with a tiny star cutter, approximately 10 mm in diameter. Hold the calyx by the stem in your left hand and roll out each petal thinly with a small glass-tipped pin. Hollow the calyx slightly. Prick a hole through the centre of the calyx and through the stem with the pin, and insert a stamen without a head, leaving a small section sticking out at the front. Secure with egg white.

Roll out a small piece of white paste until almost transparent and cut out five petals, approximately 10 mm in diameter, with a small petal cutter.

Place a petal on the palm of the hand and roll each petal until very thin and transparent with a small ball tool. Vein from the outer top edge of the petal to the point with a pin.

When all five petals have been formed in the same way arrange them on the calyx and secure with egg white. These petals should be arranged between the leaves of the calyx so that a small green star is formed in the centre. Leave to dry and dust the back of the petals with pink chalk.

Pipe a small quantity of green royal icing into the centre and insert approximately 14 stamens without tips into this. Paint the tips of the stamens with pink colouring.

Mock orange

This little flower is made in exactly the same way as the apple blossom in plate 3, with the following exceptions:

- the calyx cutter has only four points;
- there are only four white petals which are fixed onto each leaf of the calyx and not between;
- the stamens are decreased by about a half; and
- the flowers are left completely white, except for the tips of the stamens which may be painted pink.

Jasmine

Start the flowers with a Mexican hat shape in white modelling paste (see plate 3). Use the same cutter as for the anonymous flower but roll the petals into a long and pointed shape. The stem of the flower must be longer than the anonymous flower – approximately one third longer than the diameter of the flower. Hollow each petal on the back with a ball tool.

Prick through the centre and the stem with a pin, and insert a stamen with a small head, leaving about 4 mm of the stamen protruding at the top. Enlarge the hole in the centre of the flower with a No. 32 Anger modelling tool. Roll the stem between the two index fingers, moving downwards to secure the paste to the stem and tapering it slightly towards the bottom. The paste will move upwards on the stamen, eventually leaving only the protruding tip of the stamen. Leave to dry then dust the stem and the trumpet with pink chalk. Do not dust the back of the petals.

Make more flowers and make the buds as follows: Roll a tiny piece of modelling paste around a stamen dipped in egg white, a little longer than the completed flowers. Taper towards the stem end, and thicken slightly at the top, ending with a point. Leave to dry and dust with the same pink chalk.

Tape together as for the blossom (in the last paragraph).

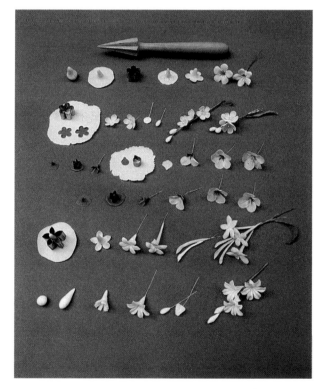

Hyacinth

Shape the required colour of modelling paste into a teardrop, with the thicker end approximately 7 mm in diameter. Press the wide end of the teardrop with the back of a small paintbrush and hollow it to form a small trumpet (see plate 3).

Make six cuts around the trumpet and cut the tip of each petal to form a point. Lie on the palm of the hand with the stem upwards, and lengthen and thin each petal with a small ball tool. Pinch and pull backwards.

Turn over and press the fluted modelling tool into the centre. Mark the veins on each petal with a pin or special veiner. Insert a stamen to form the stem

19

and press the paste firmly onto this to taper it. Leave to dry.

Make buds with a tiny piece of modelling paste. Flatten into a small triangle and place the tip of a dipped in egg white onto this. Roll into a teardrop shape that encloses the tip of the stamen. This must be about the same length as that of an individual flower petal. Dry thoroughly and tape together as for the blossoms.

The daisy

Roll the modelling paste out thinly, and cut the shape out with an eight-petalled cutter, approximately 35 mm in diameter. Cut each petal in half lengthwise, leaving the centre intact.

Spread the sixteen petals evenly in a circle, and press these flat with a No. 32 Anger tool to form the flower petals (see plate 4).

Make a small hole in the centre of the flower that will be large enough for the florist's wire later on. Place the flower on acrylic cottonwool, press with the ball end of a modelling tool to shape, and leave to dry thoroughly.

Pipe a small amount of yellow royal icing over the hole. Insert a covered No. 26 wire with a small hook at the top end and pull onto this icing.

Dust the base of the petals with green chalk. Pipe a small amount of royal icing over the hook in the centre and dip the flower into yellow nonpareils. Leave to dry.

Make a very small Mexican hat shape from green modelling paste and cut out a calyx of approximately 15 mm in diameter. Wet the back of the flower with egg white, push the stem through the calyx and secure against the flower.

Sweetpea

Special cutters to make sweetpeas are obtainable from specialist cake-decorating shops (see plate 4).

The first step in assembling this flower is to cover a short length of No. 26 florist's wire with tape (see description under *Cymbidium*). Tape a short stamen to the top end of the wire.

Roll out a small piece of prepared coloured paste very thinly and mould around the wire in a slightly rounded crescent shape.

Press out a shape in the same colour paste with a petal cutter and cut in half through the centre. Attach these two halves on either side of the crescent shape with egg white and smooth the seam at the rounded end. The straight end will be open, revealing the centre.

Cut a butterfly shape out of the paste with the se-cond cutter and lie on the palm of the hand. Thin the edges with the ball tool and ruffle. Turn over and pinch the centre on the back to form an indentation in the front. Brush this with egg white and press the modelled crescent shape flat against it. Fold slightly together to achieve a natural appearance and press to secure.

The next, slightly larger petal is cut out of thinly rolled paste with the third cutter. Ruffle and pinch on the back as for the previous petal. Wet the base of this petal with egg white and press the butterfly to the centre. Make sure that they are firmly secured and press the top of the petal over slightly to make it look soft and life-like.

To make the calyx, cut a small shape out of very thinly rolled out green modelling paste with a small star-shaped cutter, approximately 20 mm in diameter. Press the wire through the centre and secure with egg white to the bottom of the flower to form the calyx. Curl the tips back for a soft, natural appearance.

Make two more similar flowers.

Make a fourth flower by following all the steps that are mentioned above, but do not ruffle the edges of the "butterfly". (They should remain slightly flattened and secured more closely over the centre part of the flower to represent a flower which is half opened.)

Make a fifth flower, using all the illustrated stages. The layers are placed on top of each other to represent a flower that is just about to start opening. The sixth flower (a bud) is left completely closed and consists only of the rounded crescent and a petal shape that is cut with the first cutter.

Tape the bud to the top end of a No. 26 wire (covered), then tape the bud starting to open on the left. Then tape the half open flower slightly lower down on the right side of the stem. Now form a triangle with the three open flowers (two to the left and one to the right), leaving space between each flower down the stem. Finish off by covering the stalk neatly with tape.

Carnation

Roll out modelling paste very thinly and cut a scalloped shape from this with a cookie cutter (see plate 5). Make three or four shallow cuts around the edge of the scallop and a longer one of approximately 5 mm in each corner.

Use a No. 32 Anger tool or something similar in shape and roll each cut scallop with the rounded section of the cone-shaped modelling stick (roll it backwards and forwards on the same spot) to ruffle the petals. Each section must be shaped and fluted separately and must not stick to another section, so as to form individual petals.

When completely shaped and ruffled, turn upside down on the work surface. Paint egg white carefully on the unruffled centre, taking care not to wet the petals. Fold in half, pressing only on the centre of the fold. Take care not to stick the two sections together too firmly.

Push the two corners on the sides towards the middle with the end of a brush, dividing the circle into quarters. Pick the flower up in the left hand, holding only the point between the fingers. Brush some more egg white between the folds, and press together with the finger tips to form a neat round flower head.

Tape two long white stamens to the top end of a short length of No. 22 or 24 florist's wire. Press through the centre of the petals and pull through so that only the two stamens show above the petals. Press the paste firmly to the stem. If the bottom part of the flower is too long, shorten, and shape neatly and evenly around the wire stem. Leave to set thoroughly.

Cut a second pattern out of paste and follow the above procedure until the last step in the first row on the picture. In other words, do not fold together. Brush the smooth centre with egg white and insert the stem of the formed flower through the centre of the second pattern. Pleat the second row of petals around and underneath the first ones and press firmly to secure.

Trim off excess paste.

Roll out green modelling paste very thinly and cut into a rectangle with slightly slanted sides (refer to picture). Cut triangles across the upper edge of the rectangle to form the five leaves of the calyx. Roll each leaf on the underside with a ball tool to hollow slightly. Brush the uncut part with egg white, and fold around the lower half of the flower. Press firmly, and smooth the join so that it is invisible.

Cut two very tiny petal shapes out of the same green modelling paste and hollow slightly with the ball tool. Attach at the bottom of the calyx on opposite sides of the flower. Shape two more similar petals that are slightly wider and a little shorter than the first two. Attach between the other two petals on opposite sides with egg white.

Roll a tiny piece of green paste between the fingers to form a sausage that is pointed on either end and slightly thicker in the centre. Flatten slightly, stick the stem through the centre and attach to the calyx with egg white.

If the flower is to be used on a cake on its own, you can attach extra pairs of these leaves at intervals to the stem of the carnation.

Frangipani

Roll out white modelling paste to a thickness of about 1 mm and cut five petals with the frangipani cutter (see plate 5). Make sure that the rounded edge will be on your left side.

Place a petal on the palm of your hand and draw a line about 1 mm from the edge of the rounded side on the inside. Roll the edge towards you and ball with a modelling tool just inside this "roll" to cup slightly. Position diagonally over the handle of a wooden spoon, from left to right. Shape four more similar petals. Leave to set slightly (the paste must still be pliable for the next step).

Paint the lower points of the petals with yellow vegetable colouring and assemble to form a fan of overlapping petals. Press together firmly and fold the left petal over to the right, with its cupped edge just inside that of the petal on the far right. Roll the uncupped edge of the right petal over to the left, bringing it around the back of the left petal. Twist the base of the flower slightly and unfold the petals so that they curve out like a natural flower.

Wet the one end of a No. 24 florist's wire with egg white and press into the base of the flower. Secure firmly.

Put the frangipani into a cone made from a square piece of aluminium foil (cut the square through from one corner to the centre, then fold the one point over the other to form a cone). Cut a hole in the bottom of the foil and curl the edges slightly to the outside. Push the stem of the flower through the hole and place over a little spice bottle, with the stem hanging inside it. The petals should rest on the upper rounded edge of the cone.

Leave to dry and dust the inside of the petals with yellow chalk. Turn upside down and draw lengthwise veins over the petals with pinkish-brown chalk. Colour the base of the flower with brown and green chalk.

If you would like buds for your arrangement, proceed as follows:

Form an elongated teardrop over a length of covered florist's wire. Make five cuts from one point of the drop to the other around this. Holding each end between the thumb and index finger of both hands, twist the teardrop, turning the hands in opposite directions. Leave to dry.

Plate 5
How to make the
carnation (top three
lines) and the
frangipani (bottom
three lines) of
modelling paste

If you dust the centre of the flower with a darker shade of chalk before inserting the stamens you add depth to your flower.

Roll out separate pieces of white and green paste very thinly. Press the white onto the green and roll out firmly. Cut a calyx from this with a radius approximately two thirds that of the petals. Mould the tips with a ball tool (see picture).

Push the stem of the flower through the centre of the calyx and attach to the base of the flower with egg white.

Roll a small ball of green paste around the stem below the calyx to form the hip.

Cécile Brunner rose

This rose is made from three tints of the same colour (see the last three rows of plate 6, and refer to p. 16 on how to colour modelling paste).

These roses are particularly effective on christening cakes and in dainty floral arrangements. Keep them small to enable them to look as close to nature as possible. Although one can use up to twenty petals to form this rose, the diameter should not be more than 30 mm.

Use a small ball of paste in the darkest tint and shape in a sausage approximately 30 mm long and 5 mm in diameter.

Roll the sausage flat on the one side with a modelling tool until very fine and transparent. The base should remain fairly thick as this is going to form the bud of the rose. Do not allow it to become crescent shaped (refer to picture).

Bend a hook on one end of a piece of No. 24 florist's wire. Brush the lower, thick base of the rolled-out paste with egg white, put the hook on this and roll up as for a Swiss roll. The upper edge should be kept as straight as possible. Secure by pressing the thickened base firmly onto the wire. Fold the free end of the roll slightly so that it curls back.

Use the second colour to form the next three to five small petals in this way: Place a small ball of paste, approximately 4 mm in diameter, on your work surface and flatten on one side to form a rose petal shape. Mould with the ball tool until the petal is as long as the bud and very thin around the edge. This should never be longer or shorter than the bud. If you find it necessary, use a pair of scissors to trim to shape.

Lie this petal on the side of the palm of your hand, in line with the little finger, and hollow the centre with the ball tool, which will curl and ruffle the outer edge.

Brush the lower edge of the petal only with egg white and press the completed bud against the petal so that only the base is attached. It is essential that the whole upper portion of the petal is free from the bud to facilitate curling and bending. Do not turn these petals back too much at this stage as additional petals have to be attached to complete the rose.

Open rose

The rose depicted in the top two rows of plate 6 consists of five petals and the calyx.

Roll out pale pink modelling paste until almost transparent. Cut out five petals with a little cutter. Cover the balance of the rolled-out paste with a piece of plastic to prevent it from drying out.

Ruffle the outer edges of the petals with a ball modelling tool on the palm of your hand. Take care that the outer edges of the petals in particular are very thin.

Grease a table tennis ball with white vegetable fat. Press the petals against this so that the lower halves stick to the ball. The upper edges can now be curled or fluted as desired. Leave to dry.

Cut a very small calyx in the same colour paste that was used for the flowers, with the radius about one third of the length of the petals. Put in an individual polystyrene apple container and attach the dry petals to it with egg white. First overlap two petals, then attach one on the opposite side. The last two are now secured in the two spaces between the petals that have already been attached.

They should all overlap.

Pipe a small quantity of yellow royal icing in the centre where the petals meet. Insert a length of No. 22 or 24 covered florist's wire with a flattened hook at the top and pull into the royal icing.

Leave to dry.

Pipe a small quantity of yellow royal icing in a circle around the wire hook and press 45 to 50 or more artificial stamens into it. Finish off the flower neatly with a small dot of icing in the centre of the circle. Paint the tips of the stamens with brown, orange or dark-pink colouring.

Add another three to five petals in the same way in a circle around the bud to overlap each other by approximately one third. The outer petals must be made in the palest tint.

The width of the petals may differ, but they should always be of the same height otherwise the centre of the rose will be too high and the petals too low on the stem to look natural.

Never attach more than five of these petals in one stage to prevent the centre from being pressed out at the top. When you handle the flower, do not press in the centre of the petals when you attach them as this will form a little "waist" which will make the rose resemble a tulip. The flower should always be held just below the base by the stem while you work on it.

Attach the calyx when completely dry. The calyx cutter that is available for this purpose is a little clumsy for this flower. Roll out a piece of green paste very thinly until about 100 to 120 mm long and 15 mm wide. Cut into wedges as indicated in the picture and attach one by one to the base of the rose. (I usually do not curl these leaves back as their tips are inclined to break off easily. I stick them against the rose for safety's sake.)

Finally, form a very small ball of green paste of approximately 2 mm in diameter and mould it around the stem below the leaves of the calyx to form the rose hip.

Tea rose

Three tints of the same colour are used for this rose as well, but unlike the Cécile Brunner rose the starting point is a cone.

Before forming the cone decide what the size of the completed rose should be. The cone is always approximately 20 mm shorter than the actual rose. If a rose is 50 mm high, for example, the cone should not be longer than 30 mm, and the thickest point should have a diameter of about 7 mm.

The first petals are slightly thicker and narrower than the final ones, but they must all be of the same height. A templet of this petal can be cut out of wax paper and kept at hand to serve as a sample to check the height of all the following petals. Note that the petals can be gradually rolled wider.

For this rose I use three to five petals in the first colour, approximately five in the next, and as many as required in the final tint to complete the rose. There is no hard and fast rule, however, for the number differs according to size.

The tea rose is quite a heavy flower and this means using a much heavier gauge of florist's wire for the stem (No. 18 is a good thickness). The one end of the wire is turned into a hook. Form the cone around this and leave to dry thoroughly (see steps 1 and 2 on plate 7). Then attach the petals:

The first petal is formed with a very narrow tip and is about 20 mm longer than the cone. Brush the bottom edge with egg white and fold around the cone. Attach firmly at the base.

Shape the second petal and attach on the opposite side in the same way.

The third petal should be rolled slightly wider and much thinner than the first two. Lift the one side of the second petal away from the bud and insert the petal between this and the bud, as deeply as possible. Brush egg white over the bottom edge.

Shape one or two more petals and attach them in the same way. The top edges of these petals may be curled back slightly, but do not curl the first two. Leave to dry at this stage.

The next series of petals are made in the second tint of your colour. You can also use a cutter for this purpose. (I find it more satisfactory to use a piece of modelling paste shaped into a cone and then flattened and moulded into a petal with a modelling tool.) The base of these petals should be slightly thick, which ensures a good appearance.

If the dry petals make it difficult to attach the next lot, cut a crescent shape out of the lower half of the petal and insert this point between the dry petals to make it look as though this petal unfolds between the previous ones. Secure with egg white and smooth the join. It is not necessary for the last few petals to overlap each other. Curl and bend their edges to look as natural as possible.

Leave to dry completely.

Make the calyx and the rose hip as follows: Roll out a piece of white and a piece of green modelling paste thinly, place together and roll out again. Cut out the calyx and roll each leaf separately until long and very thin. Use a scalpel and make one or two cuts on the side of each leaf.

With the white uppermost, roll each leaf with a

ball tool to hollow slightly. Attach a small ball of green paste to the base of the rose. Stick the stem through the middle of the calyx and attach it to the base of the rose with egg white. Mould the calyx carefully around the piece of paste at the base of the rose to form the hip. Turn the calyx leaves over to reveal the white bloom.

Cover the wire with green paste to form the stem of the rose. Use light-brown paste and shape the thorns into a triangle, with the sharp tips slightly curved and the base fairly thick and wide. Attach to the stem with egg white.

Make the stem leaves by rolling out green modelling paste very thinly. Attach a very thin green-covered florist's wire to it with egg-white, then put a second layer of rolled-out green paste over the wire on the first layer. Use a leaf cutter and cut out. Mould the edges with a modelling stick to curl slightly, then press on an artificial or fresh leaf to create veins. Make more leaves in the same way. There should be three large ones and two slightly smaller ones.

Leave to dry completely then assemble as follows:

Use a No. 24 wire covered with florist's tape and attach one of the larger leaves to the top. Attach the two remaining large leaves opposite each other slightly lower on the stem, then the two smaller leaves lower down on the stem. Finally attach this composite leaf to the stem of the rose. You can also make another, or more, to attach to the stem.

Roll a piece of brown and a piece of green modelling paste together, cut a shape from this and attach to the base of the leaf stalk. The shape should be wider at the bottom, indented in the middle, narrow at the top, which must be cut to make it V-

shaped. Place on top of the leaf-stalk at its base, with the broader side against the flower-stalk and attach firmly with egg white.

Paint the edges of the leaves with red vegetable colouring, and dust the surface of the leaves in places with red chalk to break the green. The petals of the rose may also be dusted in places and around the edges with a deeper tint or contrasting colour to brighten it.

The tea rose can be used on its own or together with a bud and a half open rose on cakes or in arrangements. Always use odd numbers for good composition.

If you prefer, you can add a few dainty flowers like jasmine, hyacinths or blossoms.

These roses may also be tied together with ribbon made from flower paste for a softening effect, but do remember to keep to the minimum as it is the rose you want to exhibit, not the ribbon.

Cymbidium
These orchids can be made quite easily with the aid of two cutters (refer to fig. 6).

First cover a piece of No. 22 florist's wire with green florist's tape in the following way: Attach the free end of the tape firmly to the one end of the wire.

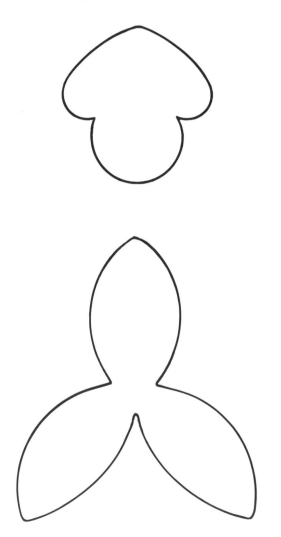

Hold the tape firmly between the thumb and index finger of the left hand, with the wire lying horizontally over the fingers and the hand (almost like a pencil). The tape will hang vertically between the fingers in the hollow of the hand. Hold the wire where the tape is attached between the thumb and index finger of the right hand and roll between these fingers. The tape should be held taut at an angle in the other hand at the same time. It will then automatically be rolled around the length of the wire in a spiral.

Bend the one end of the wire into a hook and curve about 20 mm of this end as indicated in the top line of plate 8. Mould a ball of white paste around this curve in the form of a teardrop. Pinch the rounded tip to form two tiny scallops. Flatten their edges and hollow on the inside with a ball tool. Shape the column over the fleshy part of the fingertip and allow to dry completely.

Roll a tiny piece of paste into a ball, approximately 2 mm in diameter, and attach to the front point of the column. Use a knife and divide this ball across the middle to form two "lips". Paint reddish brown dots over the surface of the hollow.

Roll out a piece of paste to an approximate thickness of 1 mm. Use the appropriate cutter and cut out (see fig. 6 and plate 8). Cut at 1 mm intervals around the lower round edge of the trumpet and ruffle using a No. 32 Anger tool (a round toothpick will also serve the purpose).

Place the trumpet on the palm of the hand and rub the rounded edges with a modelling tool until fine and slightly transparent. Roll just inside these edges with the ball of the modelling tool to cup slightly. Leave on a rounded wooden block to obtain the correct curve (these blocks are designed for making orchids and are obtainable from cake decorating shops). If you do not have one curve the trumpet over a piece of rounded tin or puffed up acrylic cottonwool.

Leave to dry completely.

Make gum paste with a little piece of modelling paste and egg white and attach to the base of the trumpet. Fix the column to this and smooth excess paste away with a fine brush. (The column fits neatly inside the trumpet.)

Roll out another piece of paste about 1 mm thick and cut out the sepals with the three-pointed cutter. Press a dried husk of maize along the length of the sepals to create veins. Lie the sepals on the palm of the hand and mould with a ball tool to thin the edge. The centre remains intact as the flower has a waxy appearance. The point of the top sepal should be modelled rounder and wider than the other two. Pinch this top point slightly to form a cup and roll lightly with a modelling tool.

Place in an individual polystyrene apple container and allow to dry. Prick a hole in the centre while still wet.

Cut out a second similar shape, but slice the top sepal to form two petals. Thin the edges with a ball tool as previously described. Again, make veins on the surface with a maize husk.

Mix a tiny ball of paste approximately 2 mm in diameter with a little egg white. Place this gum in the centre of the sepals which should still be slightly pliable.

Attach the petals to the sepals with the points upwards to form a well-balanced five-petaled shape. Curl the tips of the petals slightly forward and press the sides together lightly at the base to narrow and round them somewhat. Lift slightly by supporting them with a small piece of foam rubber or acrylic cottonwool. Prick a hole in the centre.

Place another small piece of paste mixed with egg white in the centre of the petals and pull the stem of the trumpet through so that the base is attached firmly to the petals. Smooth the excess paste away against the base of the trumpet, and support it with a piece of foam or cottonwool to prevent it sagging onto the petals. Place in a polystyrene container on top of a spice bottle, with the stem hanging into it. Leave to dry completely.

When dry, carefully lift off the bottle and paint the front edge of the trumpet with maroon to form marks typical to the *Cymbidium*. Leave to dry and then dust the whole flower with chalk to obtain a natural likeness.

Roll a piece of yellow modelling paste into a sausage with a diameter of about 3 mm. The length must be about two thirds that of the lip of the trumpet, with pointed ends. Lie a needle or pin lengthwise across this sausage and press down to form two "lips". Roll the needle slightly as well to hollow. This forms the pollinium. Attach with egg white to the throat of the trumpet.

Poorman's orchid
This pretty little orchid can be made in different colours such as red, pale mauve, pale pink, yellow and orange.

To make the trumpet roll out a piece of modelling paste so that the upper third is about twice as thick as the lower two thirds. Refer to fig. 7 on p. 26 and cut out pattern A. (The measurements in the book correspond to the natural size of the orchid.) Make sure that the leg with the rounded tip is cut out of the thicker third of the paste.

Press the other four legs with the fingers to flatten

Fig. 7
Templets for the poorman's orchid

25

Plate 8
How to make the
Cymbidium (top three
lines) and the
poorman's orchid
(bottom line) of
modelling paste

and lengthen them slightly, then use the ball tool to make them thinner. Make fine cuts on the tips of these little legs and ruffle slightly. Form them into tube-like petals by turning the sides down with a pair of tweezers. Use a toothpick and spread the ruffled edges out like a fan (see plate 8).

Pinch the paste just below the two vertical petals with the thumb and index finger or the pair of tweezers to form a "waist" with two outstretched arms and two legs – note that the legs should be parted slightly more than in the original cut-out position.

Insert a length of covered No. 26 florist's wire into the remaining rounded leg, with the tip of the wire protruding just above the two outstretched arms. Hold this section of the trumpet between the two index fingers and roll to and fro to enclose the wire by about 20 mm, tapering towards the end.

Use the sharp tip of a modelling tool and lift the paste slightly between the two vertical petals at the base of the wire. Press the tool down to make a slight hollow.

Curve the stem slightly close to the trumpet, then leave to dry.

Roll a second piece of paste out thinly, and cut out a shape with five petals with cutter B. Press all the edges with the fingers to thin them and mould lightly on the inside with a ball tool, taking care to retain the original shape of the petals. Turn upside down, place the ball of a modelling tool on the back of the top petal and ball slightly to let the petal curl over. Turn right side up and ball the other four petals in the same way. Use a pin and draw the vein from the base to the tip across the middle of each of the five petals. Handle carefully and put aside.

Make a very small ball of paste, approximately 1 mm in diameter, wet with egg white and place in the centre of these petals. Make a hole right through all the layers and wet with egg white again. Push the stem of the trumpet through this hole, taking care that about two thirds of the paste casing around the wire comes out at the bottom. Remember that the trumpet must be completely dry. Smooth the excess paste from the ball against the upper third of the casing.

Put the stem down flat on a piece of polystyrene and support the flower with pieces of foam rubber to retain the shape of the orchid. Allow to dry completely.

Pipe two dots on either side of the indentation at the base of the two vertical "arms" of the trumpet with a No. 1 writing tube and bright yellow royal icing. Pipe a third and slightly elongated nodule between them a little lower down.

Finally, paint a white dot on the little tip protruding above the identation and the three yellow markings.

This orchid can be used on its own or in an arrangement with larger orchids.

Moth orchid

This is one of the most difficult but most rewarding orchids to make.

The trumpet is made first. Cut a piece of No. 24 florist's wire into a length of approximately 100 mm and cover it with florist's tape as described under the *Cymbidium*. Bend the tip of this wire around the fleshy part of the tip of the index finger so that it forms a semicircle from the one end of the nail to the other end (it should have a diameter of about 15 mm).

Mould a ball of white modelling paste (approximately 4 mm in diameter) around the wire semicircle, forming a little "lip" or projection on the bend between the semicircle and the length of the stem (see plate 9). Allow to dry.

Roll out a piece of paste to a thickness of about 1 mm and cut it out with the appropriate cutter (see fig. 8) to obtain a trumpet pattern. Ball the elongated sharp tip of the trumpet to thin it out. Make an incision lengthwise down the centre of the elongated part of the trumpet as shown on the photograph (see example 2 in the second row). Roll each "feeler" to and fro between the thumb and index finger and roll around a toothpick to curl.

Pinch the back of the trumpet from the base of the feelers to just below the two side petals. This will form a vein in the front and make the sides turn slightly inwards.

Use a ball tool and thin out the two petals at either side of the centre point to enlarge them. Place on the palm of the hand and ball slightly in the centre to cup each petal.

Leave the small straight portion intact, but brush egg white from the tip to the middle of the trumpet between the two side petals. Attach the prepared hook. Arrange the petals and feelers to shape the trumpet. Place in one of the hollows of an ice-ball tray (diameter: 20 mm) and leave to dry. This will ensure that the trumpet will hold its shape.

Make a ball of yellow modelling paste, approximately 4 mm in diameter. Pinch on one side between two fingers to form a triangle, and make an incision with a knife on the top flat side to form two "lips" that are slightly parted. Cut the sharp tip of the triangle away with a pair of scissors, brush with egg white and attach inside the trumpet at the base of the paste-covered hook.

Roll a piece of white paste until thin and transparent. Cut two petals out of it (see centre diagram on fig. 8). Please note, they should be mirror images of each other, in other words first use the one side of the cutter, turn over and use the other

Fig. 8.
Templets to make the moth orchid (these as well as the previous two sets are not available in the shops and must be made specially)

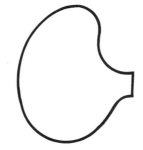

Plate 9
The moth orchid

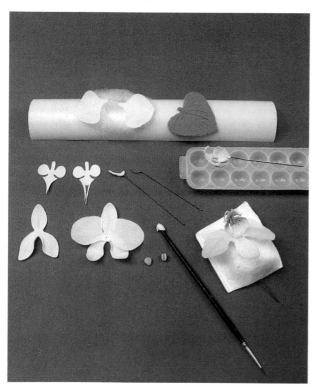

side. Thin these petals out with a roller, especially around the edges to make them very transparent. Vein by pressing the stem-leaf of a violet onto them (an artificial rubber leaf may also be used for this purpose). Place on acrylic cottonwool over a rolling pin or on the round part of a piece of corrugated fibreglass. Take care that the petals do not curl up, but remain stretched out like the wings of a moth. Leave to dry thoroughly.

Next cut out the sepals with a third cutter (see end diagram on fig. 8). Vein each sepal with a piece of dried husk of maize as described for the *Cymbidium*. Use a ball tool and roll the back of the top sepal just above its base to cup slightly. Turn over and cup the tip of the top sepal (in the front) in the same way. Repeat this step to curl the edges and tips of the last two sepals.

Cut out an individual container from a polystyrene fruit tray and turn upside down. Place the sepals against it, with the largest portion resting flat against the side of the container – just the two bottom tips will curl up slightly.

Cover a very tiny ball of paste with egg white and press this "gum" in the centre where the sepals meet. Attach the petals (see example 2 in the bottom row of plate 9). Press another piece of modelling paste over the join and brush with egg white. Prick a hole right through all the layers, including the polystyrene, and push the stem with the trumpet attached to the top through this hole. Pull tightly against the petals and into the paste. Work the excess paste neatly away with a brush. Leave to dry.

Roll a small peace of white paste on the palm of your hand to form a teardrop. The wider part of the

Plate 10
How to make a swan
with flood icing

teardrop should be approximately 5 mm in diameter. Use a small pair of scissors and halve the drop from the sharp tip to approximately 5 mm from the rounded head. Stick the back of a paintbrush into the head between the two halves. Cut the left half into a small V-shaped lip. Then roll the shaft to and fro on the right half to hollow. Cut a piece off the latter so that it will be about 10 mm long from its end to the rounded tip of the head (the distance between the point of the V and the rounded tip of the head is approximately 7 mm). Fit this little "hood" over the protruding tip at the base of the trumpet (attach with egg white). Smooth the paste neatly with the brush to bind the component parts together.

Allow to dry thoroughly and paint three dotted maroon lines from the base towards the outer edges of the left and right petals of the trumpet. The centre line should be slightly longer than the other two. Paint little dots in the same colour on the pollinium and draw lines across the little stem of the trumpet.

Dust the inner third of the trumpet around the pollinium with yellow chalk and colour the protruding node with rose pink.

Flood work

Swan

Although the body of the swan is flat and in one solid piece, one should work carefully to capture the gracefulness of the bird.

Secure a piece of wax paper over the traced pattern and pipe the outlines with royal icing (see plate 10). Pipe the flood icing into the space between the lines and use a brush to paint the icing towards and onto the outlines as described on p. 14 to 15. Start at the head and gradually fill the neck and then the body until the whole is completed. Leave to dry thoroughly.

To lift the swan from the wax paper, remove the thumb tacks or Sellotape, hold a light flat board horizontally against the one on which the swan was made, pull the end of the wax paper through the slit between the two boards and keep on pulling until the swan has gradually moved from the one board and slipped onto the other. Or use a spatula with a very thin blade to loosen the swan from the wax paper. A length of taut cotton thread may also be inserted between the swan and the wax paper and then gradually pulled from one side to the other to loosen the swan.

Turn the swan over onto its flooded side. Do not outline again, but flood as described above. Brush the flood icing very carefully onto the outer edges, but take care that it does not overflow. When dry, the seam will be hardly visible. Put aside and make the wings.

Starting at the tip, pipe the top outline using a No. 1 writing tube with royal icing, and then pipe a series of lines close together using the same icing and

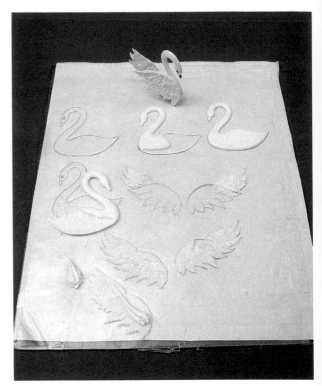

tube. Use a brush to fill in any spaces between the lines. Pipe two more similar rows of lines as depicted in the photograph to form feathers and complete the main section of the wing by again piping three layers of lines in a similar fashion. Leave to dry thoroughly and in the meantime form another wing which will be a mirror image of the first one (see plate 10).

Use a No. 5 star tube for assembling the different components. Pipe a pear-shaped support, push the breast of the swan into the wide end and position neatly. (Please note, at this stage the eyes and the beak should already have been painted.) Allow to dry.

Remove the wings from the wax paper as described above, turn upside down and pipe an elongated pear shape, from the rounded end towards the pointed tip (with a No. 5 star tube and royal icing). Attach these wings at an angle on either side of the breast of the swan and support with small pieces of foam rubber in order to dry in the correct position.

Angels or cherubs

These angels (plate 11 and fig. 32) are more difficult to flood than the swan as they are built up in four different stages.

A close examination of the picture reveals that the wings are situated behind the body (mark as No. 1). The one leg crosses over the other (mark them respectively No. 2 and 1). The head fits onto the body (mark them 3 and 2) and then finally number the loin-cloth No. 4, as this will be flooded last. Proceed as follows:

Pipe the wings as described for the swan, using a single layer only. Start just inside the lines of the body and the arms, and work towards the outer edges of the wings. When the wings have been

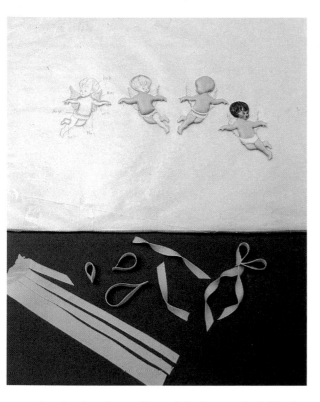

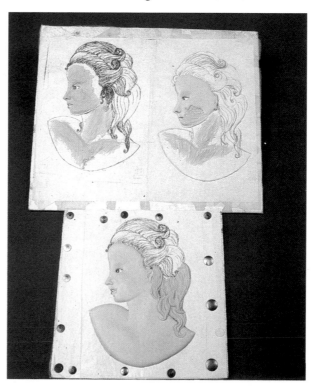

Plate 11
Angels in flood icing
(top) and ribbons of
modelling paste
(bottom)

completed, pipe the outline of the leg marked No. 1 with flesh-coloured royal icing and a No. 1 tube. Fill in with flood icing in the same colour as described on p. 14 to 15. This leg should not be too high, otherwise the second leg, when completed, will appear to be out of proportion.

Outline the body and arms and take care to pipe the lines *over* the wings. Fill with flood icing. Then complete the second leg as follows: Pipe a short line from the foot at the back up to the loin-cloth and then from the foot down towards the ankle of the leg in front. Pipe a similar line from the already-formed thigh down towards the unformed knee. Then pipe the whole of the outline of the leg in front (over the leg at the back and the lines just completed). This prevents the leg in front from sagging unnaturally in places. Fill in with flood icing.

Pipe the outline of the head (yet again overlapping the neck of the torso) and flood. Lastly outline the loin-cloth (over the waist and legs) and flood.

Because the head of the angel is so small components such as the hair, cheeks and nose are not built up. These are eventually completed by painting with vegetable colouring.

Hint: Always try to make more than one angel at a time to ensure that, when moving over from one numbered section to another, the previous section will be dry before the one overlapping it is flooded.

Arrange in pairs on top of or around the side of a cake and link together with garlands of flowers and/or ribbons (refer to plate 30).

Cameo

Although this pattern appears to be very easy, the flood-work technique requires a reasonable measure of skill, because the cameo is usually made in a single colour. The icing should, therefore, be applied to form shadows and highlights by building up the natural contours of the bust.

Begin by using flesh-coloured royal icing in a piping bag without a tube. Cut an opening at the tip about the size of a No. 2 tube. Pipe icing over the eyebrow-ridge and, using a brush, smooth the icing down towards the hair line and the bridge of the nose, the eyelids and the temple. Build up the cheek, nose and chin in a similar manner. (There must be hollows between the eye and the temple, along the nose, next to the cheek and around the mouth.) Also build up the section over the neck, from the ear to the collar-bone, and from shoulder to shoulder to form the two collar-bones.

Pipe a line with a No. 1 writing tube from the collar-bone over the neckline to just above the shoulder line (flatten the ends). Pipe a similar line, flattened at both ends, over the jaw line (see first example on plate 12).

Pipe the outline of the bust by starting at the neck line and finishing below the ear. The second line will stretch from the jaw over the already-piped line of the neck to the collar-bone. The third line will stretch around the face and over the already-piped line of the jaw line. Outline the eye. Flood the whole by starting at the top, gradually working down towards the jaw. Take special care at the jaw and neck lines to ensure that the correct parts are rounded.

Like the feathers of the swan, the curls of hair are built up in stages, working from below upwards using flesh-coloured royal icing, a No. 1 writing tube and a paintbrush. Lastly form the eye and lips with flesh-coloured flood icing.

Plate 12
Cameo

Plate 13
Little fisherman

Attach a piece of rolled-out, oval-shaped reddish-brown or royal-blue fondant with egg white to the top of the cake and fit the bust to it. Or mount the bust directly onto an oval cake that has been covered with reddish-brown or royal-blue fondant. Finish the cameo off by piping a frame with a No. 2 writing tube around the oval (you may use white royal icing for this purpose). Allow to dry and paint the frame gold. (See completed cake on plate 43.)

Little fisherman

As is customary, the first step is to number the different components chronologically, working from below upwards. Here it is as follows:

1 the face, the crown of the hat, the part of the shirt underneath the sleeve, and the inside of the trousers at the back where the one brace ends;
2 the neck and back of the shirt;
3 the hair;
4 the trousers and continuous bottom brace;
5 the piece of shirt showing under the top brace and the brim of the hat;
6 the seat of the trousers above the handkerchief;
7 the top brace;
8 the left-hand part of the handkerchief;
9 the part of the handkerchief in the three-o'clock to five-o'clock position;
10 the pocket on the seat of the trousers;
11 the piece of the handkerchief just to the left of the one mentioned under No. 9;
12 the last part of the handkerchief; and
13 the hat-band.

Please note, as mentioned on p. 15, the little boy may be built up three-dimensionally. Therefore, trace the legs, arm and hat-band onto a separate piece of greaseproof paper (see plate 13 and compare the completed cake on plate 38). Outline these and flood – in the case of the legs, first the feet and then the trouser-legs. Allow to dry.

Meanwhile, build up the face of the boy with flesh-coloured royal icing as described for the cameo. The eyebrow-ridge, tip of the nose, cheek, lips and ear-lobe must be rounded and the eye-socket, ear-hole, mouth and the space between the cheek and the nose indented. Allow to dry and, if necessary, correct parts that are too rounded by sandpapering them flatter. It is also not too late to build up parts that are too flat with additional royal icing. Pipe the outline of the face and flood.

Complete the rest of the boy step by step, taking special care when forming the crown of the hat: Only outline the left and right panels; then flood and allow to dry. Then pipe a blue line from panel to panel, approximately 1 mm lower than the top line of the hat-band. Flood *without* piping lines for the middle panel. Just push the icing against the outer edge of the previous panels. In this way a natural crease will be obtained.

When completely dry, paint the face and paint little white dots on the shirt, sleeve, handkerchief and hat-band. Pipe white stitches along the creases of the hat with white royal icing and a No. 0 writing tube. Lastly attach the brim of the hat (flooded separately) along the lower edge of the hat-band with royal icing to stand away slightly from the face.

Assemble on the cake as depicted on plate 38. Roll a piece of fondant in blue out thinly and cut to form a pool of water. Attach with royal icing to the cake. Make the rocks as explained on p. 32 and arrange around the banks of the pool. The rock on which the little boy is sitting is made of fondant.

The individual sections of the boy are attached section by section with royal icing: first the body, then the arms and the legs. The fishing-rod made of modelling paste is then placed between the hands, with the rod extending over the hip where it is attached to the body (a clever piece of camouflage!)

Attach the tin with bait, the fish and the frog (all separately flooded), and form a fishing-line with black royal icing and a No. 1 writing tube. Also form tufts of reeds from vermicelli and royal icing (first colour and attach the former, and then make seed-pods with brown royal icing and a No. 1 writing tube).

To make sand and gravel, crush rocks of sugar with a rolling-pin and press in on the foreground: Dilute royal icing with water until liquid, brush over the demarcated area and sprinkle with the gravel.

To complete the cake, paint clouds in the sky with vegetable colouring and shade the water surface so that it does not appear too flat and blue.

The side of the cake may be left undecorated or have only a few decorations as simplicity is the decisive factor – too much ornamentation will draw attention away from the main design on top of the cake and be excessive.

Santa Claus

Build up the face with royal icing in flesh colour as previously described. Build up the bulge where the cap is creased on the left side of the face (in red) in the same way. Pipe two short lines on top of each other, tapering at both ends, along the edge of the crease. Outline the cap, starting from the lower edge of the crease, over the two lines already piped. Note that the outline should wave slightly where the sideburn shows on the side of the face (see plate 14, first step).

Flood the cap, starting from the side of the face, tapering slightly towards the crease in the cap. Complete flooding, taking care that the flood icing will not overflow where the crease was built up. This method will result in a natural-looking crease. Then outline and flood the semicircle of the cap peeping out at the top of the head behind the fur.

Then outline the eyes and the whole of the face, starting from the nostril, along the line below the

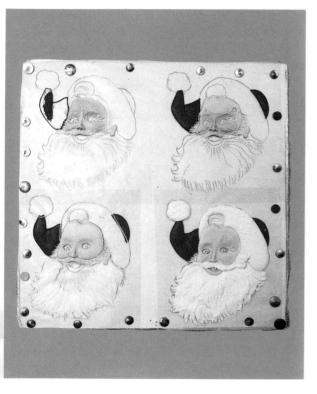

cheek. Start flooding from the hair line down towards the cheek line. Take special care around the eyes. Leave to dry thoroughly and then pipe the sideburn on the left cheek over the cap.

Pipe the beard with white royal icing in a No. 1 writing tube (refer to the method used for making the wing of the swan and the hair of the cameo). Build up the beard slightly just below the lower lip to make the centre higher than the sides and the tips. Work slightly over the outline for the lower lip so that this outline, when piped, will lie over the beard.

Leave to dry thoroughly.

Outline the lip in flesh colour, and flood. Leave this to dry. Use a brush with a small quantity of flood icing and fill in the tongue.

Pipe the outlines for the fur on the cap (see step 3 on the photograph), and flood. Pipe the sideburn on the right side of the face as well as the quiff on the forehead. Also complete the pompon on the tip of the cap.

Pipe the moustache over the upperlip and fill the eye-sockets with white royal icing. Leave to dry, and pipe the eyelids in flesh-coloured royal icing in a No. 0 writing tube.

Dip the brush in white flood icing and dab this over the fur of the cap to make it look fluffy.

Lastly paint the pupils, the eye-lashes, the lip, the cheeks and the tip of the nose to your liking, and then pipe the bushy eyebrows with white royal icing in a No. 1 writing tube.

Collars

At the back of the book you will find about half a dozen patterns for collars which may be used on a wide range of cakes (see fig. 25 to 31). A rule of thumb to be considered at this stage is that, in the case of collars overlapping the edge of the cakes, best results will be obtained with cakes with a diameter of between 20 and 25 cm. The diameter can of course be larger should you want the outer edge of the collar to rest on the edge of the cake.

However, for collar work the flood icing should not be too thick. I prefer a consistency based on the measure of seven counts (refer to the recipe on p. 14). Do not overfill the pattern with flood icing – this will result in the design looking heavy and clumsy.

In the case of floral pattern (refer to plate 47 and the corresponding fig. 30) the system of numbering, of which the little fisherman on p. 30 is an excellent example, should be followed. That is, the flowers should be flooded in small stages to prevent them from flowing into one another. The same principle applies to collars with multiple levels (compare the 60th anniversary cake, plate 49).

If the collar is bordered on the inner or outer edge with a strip or band, you must flood it first and only do the detail work or filigree once it has dried, to achieve an even whole. Before flooding the border band the outlines should be piped with royal icing and a No. 1 writing tube. Then flood as follows:

Start at a certain point, flooding 5 cm to the left and then 5 cm to the right; then continue with 5 cm to the left and 5 cm to the right. Repeat until completed. Should you follow a different procedure by working in one direction only, the join will be visible as the icing will have formed a crust by the time you finish.

Be very careful not to leave little air bubbles in the flood icing. Should any appear, break them immediately by pricking with a needle or the point of

Plate 14
Santa Claus

31

a brush, and smooth. If you don't do this, they may burst at a later stage and leave unsightly holes when the collar is completed and dry.

Hint: To ensure that the flood icing is level and even tap the glass or board on which you are working on the table every now and then and place the finished article under a strong light or in front of a fan heater. This forms a crust quickly and makes the appearance smooth and shiny.

To obtain a neat and continuous line, for instance the inside line of the christening cake on plate 31, place the pattern (secured on glass or a wooden board under wax paper) on a turntable. Hold the icing bag in your right hand, with the elbow propped up on the table, and place the point of the writing tube on the pattern. Exert pressure on the icing bag while lifting the hand a few centimetres above the work surface. Hold the hand in this position while you maintain an even pressure on the bag and turn the turntable slowly with the left hand. This produces an even outline with only one join.

Miscellaneous decorations

Lace work
Lace patterns are also to be found at the back of the book (see fig. 9). It is advisable to fill a whole sheet of these individual motifs at one time, as large quantities are usually attached to cakes. Trace the patterns very neatly onto greaseproof paper and secure on a board under wax paper or under glass and proceed as follows:

Using a No. 0 writing tube and royal icing, pipe each motif neatly and accurately. Leave on the wax paper or glass to dry thoroughly and store until required. Lift each piece very carefully off the paper or glass and attach to the cake with royal icing.

Borders and embroidery
See fig. 10 to 24 for patterns for this type of decoration. A No. 0 and/or 1 writing tube is usually used. If possible, pipe this free-hand on the cake with the pattern as guide. A beginner will, however, find the tracing method more preferable:

Determine the circumference of the cake and add 20 mm at both ends. Also measure the height of the cake and cut a corresponding strip of wax paper to fit neatly around the cake. Then decide how many times the pattern should be repeated (for example eight times). Fold the paper in half, again in half and then once more in half. Trace the pattern on the upper section of the folded paper, trace hard to ensure that the design will show through all the layers. When you unfold the paper, the pattern will be evenly distributed. Wrap around the cake and pinprick the design onto the side of the cake on the fondant.

Pipe the design with royal icing over these marks,

keeping the original pattern at hand to refer to where the pinpricks are a little faint.

Paste ribbon
The basis for this is modelling paste (see recipe p. 15), mixed with a small amount of extra gum powder for greater elasticity and strength.

Roll the paste out until paper thin and transparent, then cut even strips, using a parsley cutter. For a finer or a narrower ribbon, these strips may be halved lengthwise.

Fold loops to form the bow when you assemble them eventually. Pinch a reasonable portion of the end together and leave to dry as depicted on plate 11. Also shape the ends of the bows by curling and twisting them slightly. Use royal icing to assemble the bow. An example in using the ribbons can be seen on plate 30.

Should you want your ribbon to be glossy, brush with a glaze made of gum acacia powder (see recipe below). One layer will give you a very slight sheen, two or more will give you a high gloss. The layers should be left to dry before applying one over the other.

60 g gum acacia or gum arabic powder
125 ml cold water

Dissolve the gum in the water over a low temperature until completely melted and clear. Strain through a muslin cloth and store in the fridge in a screw-top jar. A few drops of brandy may be added to prevent the glaze from going off.

Sugar rocks
1 kg granulated sugar
250 ml cold water
½ x recipe royal icing (see p. 14)

Melt the sugar in the water over a low temperature and boil to 138 °C (280 °F). Remove from the stove and immediately stir in the very well beaten royal icing. Pour into a shoe box or something similar, lined with well-greased wax paper. The mixture will bubble up to double its original volume. Leave to cool and then break up into required sizes (rocks).

To obtain coloured rocks, colour the royal icing beforehand.

For sand and gravel, crush the rocks with a rolling pin.

Glitter
Prepare the glaze mixture as described under paste ribbon above. Brush this mixture onto a clean porcelain or enamel surface. Dry in an oven at a low temperature. As soon as it is dry, remove from the oven and flake off. Store in an air-tight jar.

For coloured glitter, mix colouring into the liquid glaze mixture before drying.

If you would like glitter on a Christmas tree or another object, the flakes can be crushed and the object dusted with it.

Rice-paper painting

Patterns for flood work (see fig. 32 to 44), as well as more detailed pictures are suitable for rice-paper painting. The technique is as follows:

Place the rice paper with the smooth side upwards over the pattern to be used. Trace every detail with a very fine felt-tipped pen. Brush this side with clear piping gel, using a No. 10 flat-tipped brush, applying even strokes in one direction. Do not criss-cross the gel over the design. The layer of gel should be very thin and extend about 5 cm beyond the outer edges of the pattern. (Incidentally, the gel is easily obtainable on the market.) Paint the picture with vegetable colouring while the gel is still wet, and allow to dry. See to it that there are shades and highlights to obtain depth and dimension.

Cut out carefully, leaving a frame of about 2 mm right round the picture. Turn over and cover the rough side of the rice paper with piping gel (once again with even strokes of the brush). Position the gelled side on the cake and press carefully with the handle of the brush to secure (only along the edge – do not press the centre as this could result in the rice paper tearing and spoiling the picture).

Cakes for special occasions

Plate 15
An engagement cake
depicting the three
stages of courting

The first step in sugar art is to learn how to cover a cake neatly with almond paste and fondant. This aspect has been covered in the chapter with recipes. The second step is mastering the technique of making flowers and miscellaneous decorations and doing flood work, which has been covered in the previous chapter in detail.

It is, however, not enough to be efficient with modelling tools and icing tubes – one should be able to assemble the individual components to form a pleasing and well finished whole. On the following pages you will find approximately 33 full-colour illustrations of examples of completed cakes for special occasions.

Plate 16
A close-up of the
young man asking the
girl for her hand in
marriage

Plate 17
An unusual wedding
cake with collar and
sweetpeas, suitable for
a small reception (see
fig. 28 and 29 for
patterns of the collars)

Plate 18
A round wedding cake decorated with sprays of *Cymbidiums*, poorman's orchids, anonymous flowers, white blossoms and gypsophila (see fig. 19 for a pattern of the border)

Plate 19
A close-up of the orchid spray on the round wedding cake

Plate 20
A light-blue oval wedding cake, delicately decorated with
fragile pink open roses, blossoms and anonymous flowers (see
fig. 11 for a pattern of the border)

Plate 21
A close-up of a spray on the oval cake

Plate 22 (left)
A white square wedding cake decorated with daisies of modelling paste. The border (see fig. 18 for a pattern) is done in pale yellow and pale green royal icing to blend with the colour scheme of the modelled decorations

Plate 23
A white six-sided wedding cake decorated with moth orchids, hyacinths and daisies. The main colours are white and yellow, which are repeated on the border (see fig. 10 for a pattern of the latter)

Plate 24
A close-up of the arrangement on the top layer of the six-sided cake

Plate 25 (left)
A pale pink scalloped
wedding cake
decorated with apple
blossoms, jasmine and
Cécile Brunner roses

Plate 26
A close-up of the
decoration on the top
layer of the scalloped
cake

Plate 27
A close-up of the side
view of the scalloped
cake

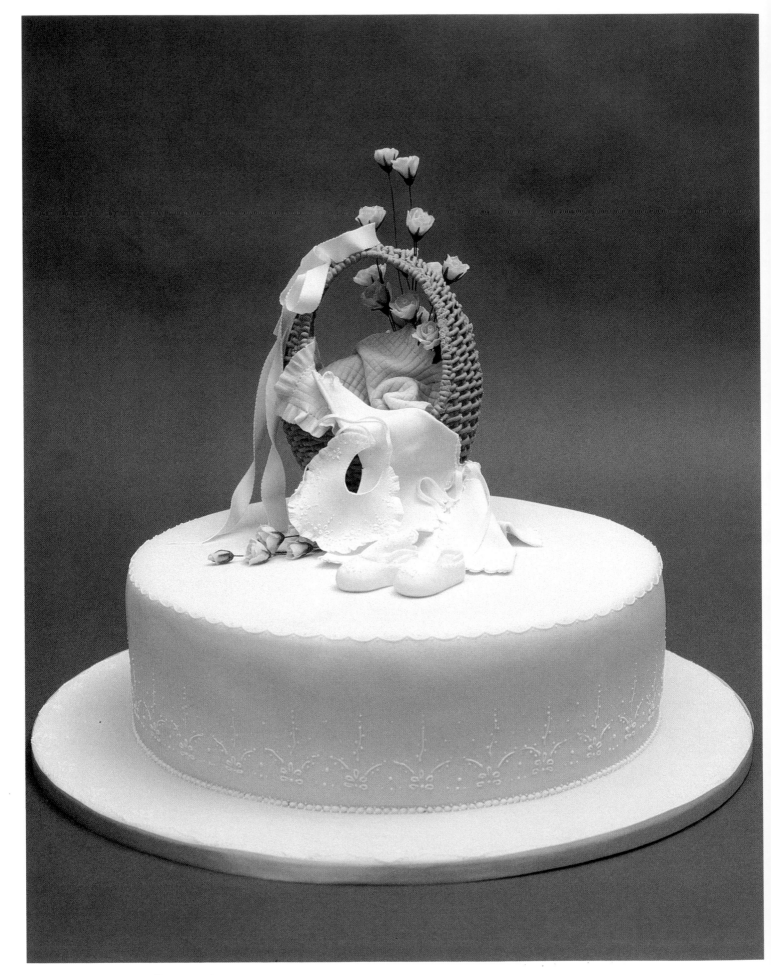

Plate 28 (left)
A christening cake with basket, baby blanket, bib, matinée jacket and bootees, finished off with paste ribbons, yellow Cécile Brunner roses and lace work (see fig. 13 for a pattern)

Plate 29
For balance, rhythm and composition the central motif of this christening cake is complemented with Cécile Brunner roses, anonymous flowers, paste ribbons, cherubs and delicate blossoms

Plate 30
A close-up of the side view of the christening cake with babe

Plate 31
A christening cake decorated with an unusual collar (see fig.
26) and flood work (see fig. 34)

Plate 32
This birthday cake for a toddler is a clear example of the successful blending of different decorating techniques: the clock-case is cut out of modelling paste to which extra powdered gum was added and the face out of fondant; the pendulums and mouse are made of modelling paste and the roses and forget-me-nots of royal icing

Plate 33
A fantasy cake for an infant's birthday party

Plate 34
A square cake for Mother's Day or for a little girl's birthday. It is
decorated with flood work and Cécile Brunner roses

Plate 35
The striking aspect of this birthday cake for a girl is the double collar (see fig. 25 with its caption). Both the cake and board were first covered with fondant, after which the outlines of the scallops were pinpricked onto the board and then piped with royal icing and a No. 1 writing tube. The two collars were flooded separately, attached to each other and then attached to the cake after the flood work had been done

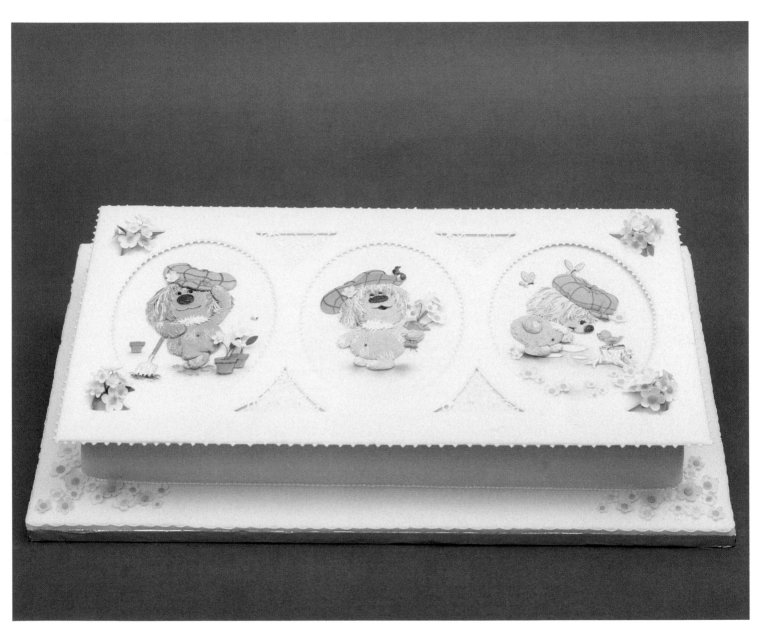

Plate 36
A birthday cake decorated with characters from the fantasy
world of the infant. It was awarded the first prize at the 1983
Cape Show and was made by Cynthia Fletcher, a student of
the author

Plate 37
A close-up of the cake on p. 49

Plate 38
The little fisherman (see fig. 38 for a pattern and p. 30 for the instructions)

Plate 39
A birthday cake for a male who has an interest in sport. The
rice-paper technique was followed here (see p. 33). Note,
however, that the pattern (fig. 44) may also be flooded

Plate 40
A birthday cake for a bridge enthusiast. Extra powdered gum was added to the modelling paste for the cards, book, pencil, cigarettes and ashtray, but note that the motifs on the cards were painted onto rice paper (if preferred, they may be flooded)

Plate 41
A relief cake for a man or a lady (the pattern, fig 40, is to be
found at the back of the book). Follow the method of the
cameo as set out on p. 29 for the flood work

Plate 42
For this cake Cynthia Fletcher was awarded the prize for the
most outstanding cake on the Cape Show of 1983

Plate 43 (left)
The cameo (see fig. 39 for the pattern and p. 29 for the instructions)

Plate 44
A 21st birthday cake for a girl. The Cécile Brunner roses, carnations, daisies and blossoms of modelling paste vary in shades from pale pink and lilac to white. The parasol is also made of modelling paste and shaped over a rubber ball just larger than a tennis ball. For the greeting card extra powdered gum was added to the modelling paste, which was then rolled out, cut and curled. For patterns of the flood work (key) and border see fig. 35 and 21 respectively (note that the basket of the latter was converted into an umbrella)

Plate 45
Cynthia Fletcher was awarded another first prize for this 21st
birthday cake at the Cape Show of 1983

Plate 46
A Mother's Day cake decorated with hyacinths, anonymous flowers and small *Cymbidiums*, varying in shade from deep cream to almost rust-brown. The border is unusual in the sense that it runs around the cake at an angle of 45° (see crease indication on fig. 14), i.e. one half should rest on the board

Plate 47
Doily collar (see fig. 30 for pattern) with a repetition of the
design of the collar on the board. The rose motif is repeated
free-hand with a No. 1 writing tube in pale green and pale pink
around the lower border of the cake

Plate 48
A cake in the shape of a horse shoe for a 25th wedding
anniversary. The frangipani arrangement is finished off with
paste ribbons (turn to fig. 22 for the pattern of the border)

Plate 49
A birthday or wedding anniversary cake. The figures and
decorations may be altered to suit different occasions (see fig.
27 for the pattern of the collar)

Plate 50
Santa Claus (see fig. 42 for a pattern for flooding and p. 31 for
the instructions)

Plate 51
A Christmas cake with a square collar (see fig. 31 for the pattern)

Plate 52
A round Christmas cake with a flood work motif (see fig. 41 for the pattern). The border is finished off with half bells, holly leaves and berries

Plate 53
Close-up of the bell border motif (the bells are shaped in a plastic mould for modelling paste and cut in half before the paste is completely dry)

Plate 54
A Christmas cake with a round collar. The mock orange blossoms, holly leaves and berries are made of modelling paste. The candle is made with royal icing and a No. 8 Tala tube (remark: cutters for holly leaves are obtainable from cake decorating shops)

Plate 55
Close-up of the border of the round Christmas cake. The leaves are made of royal icing using an icing bag cut according to fig. 3, while a No. 1 writing tube is used for the berries and stems

Plate 56 (right)
A Christmas cake with choir boys and a lamp post of modelling paste. The Christmas tree was made separately using the same method as for the wings of the swan (refer to p. 28), with the difference that the front is left to dry and then the process is repeated on the other side

Plate 57
This is not a cake in
the true sense of the
word, but a very good
example of the
versatility of sugar art

Patterns

The beginner does not always find it easy to acquire patterns for sugar art. For this reason I have provided a selection of examples of the cream of my collection.

Lace work

Fig. 9

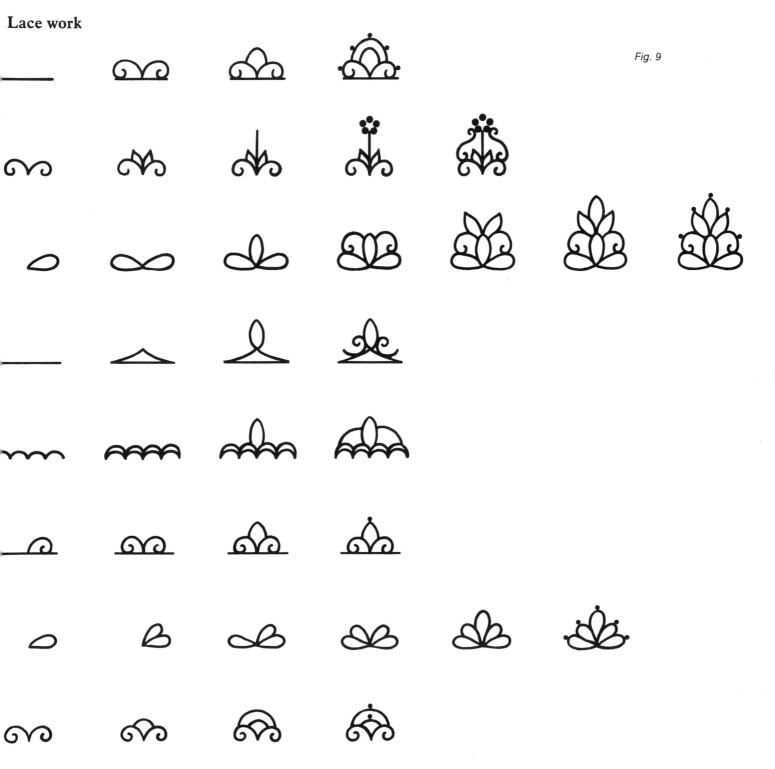

Borders

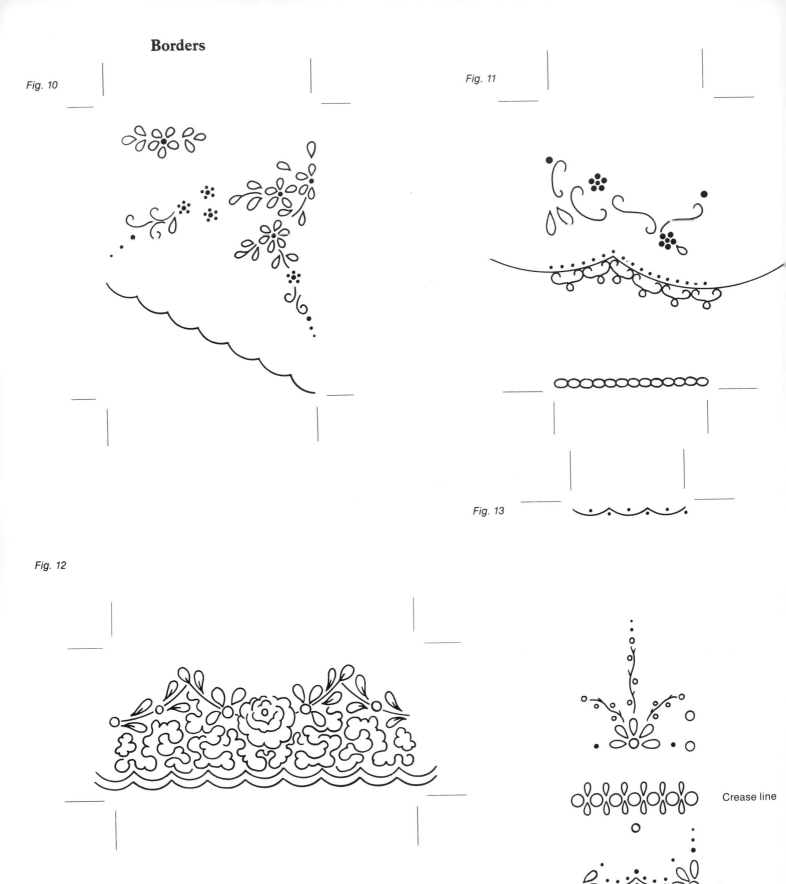

Fig. 10

Fig. 11

Fig. 13

Fig. 12

Crease line

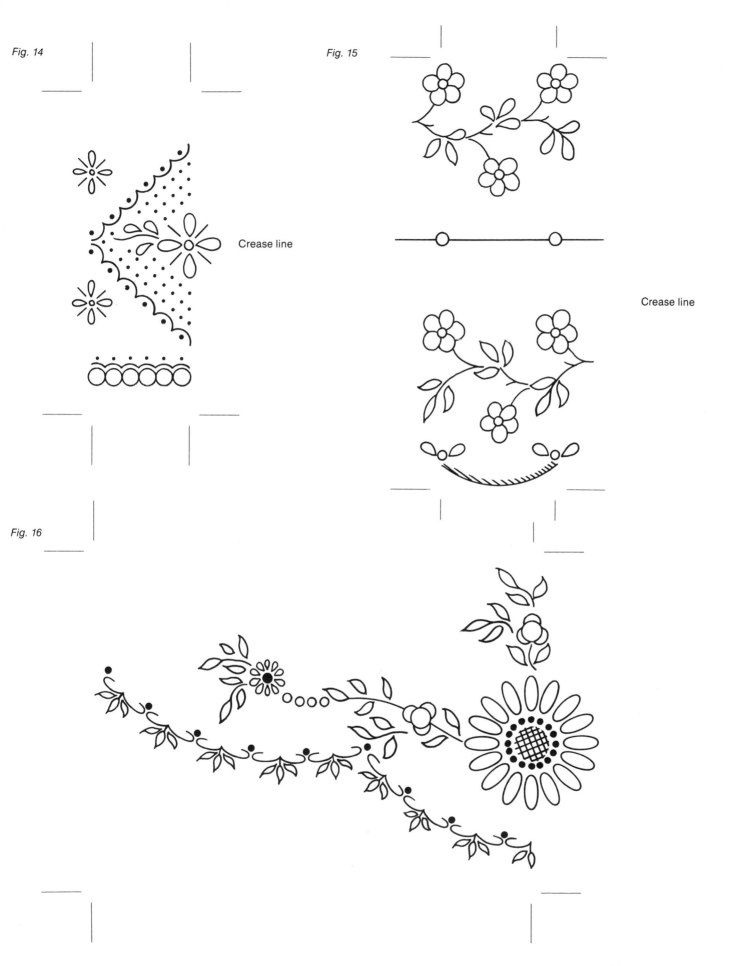

Fig. 14

Crease line

Fig. 15

Crease line

Fig. 16

Fig. 17

Fig. 18
Please note when
making the dots, they
should decrease in
size from the inside to
the outside

Fig. 19

Fig. 20

Crease line

Fig. 21

Fig. 22

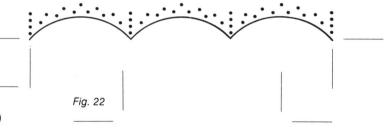

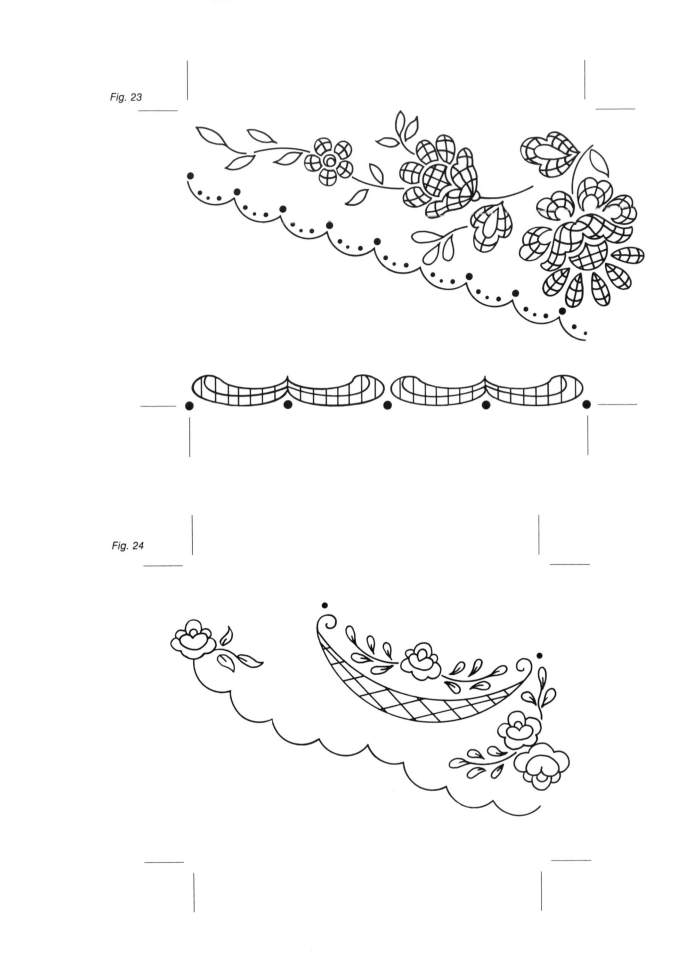

Fig. 23

Fig. 24

74

Collars

Fig. 25
This is a double collar. The inside line of the collar and the scalloped outline should be traced to form a solid collar and flooded as a whole; then the inside line of the circle and the second-last scalloped line of the collar, with all the filigree designs, should be traced and flooded as the second collar

Fig. 26

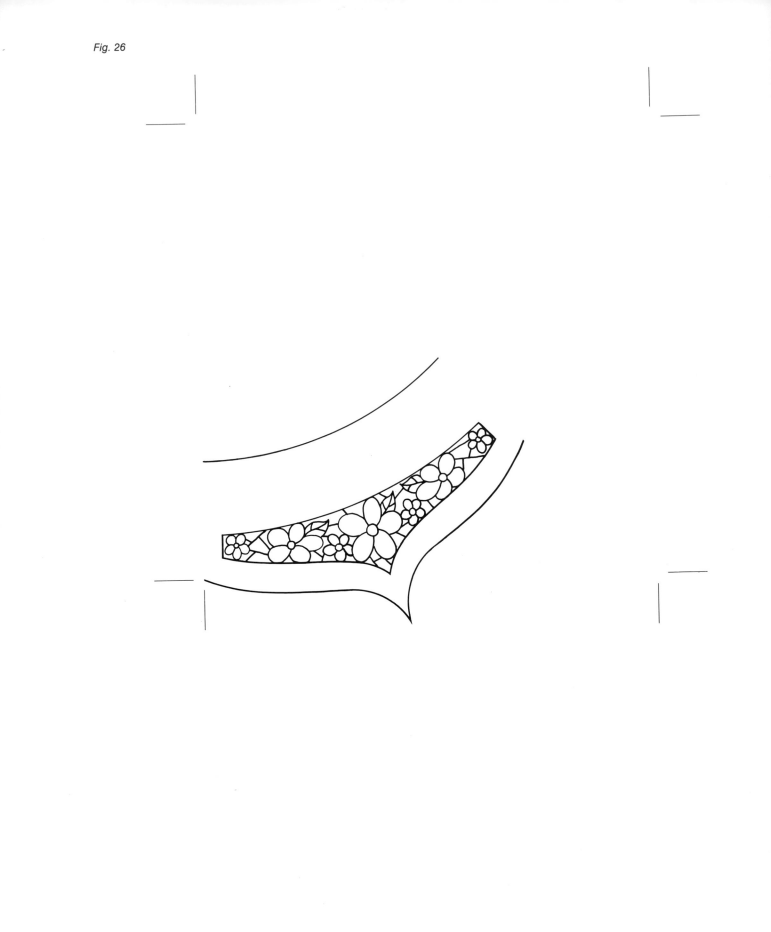

Fig. 27

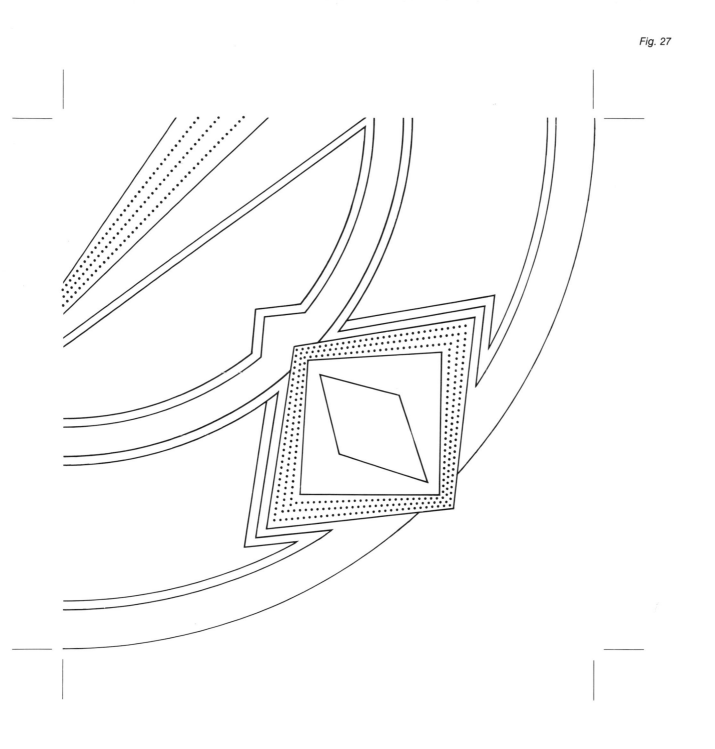

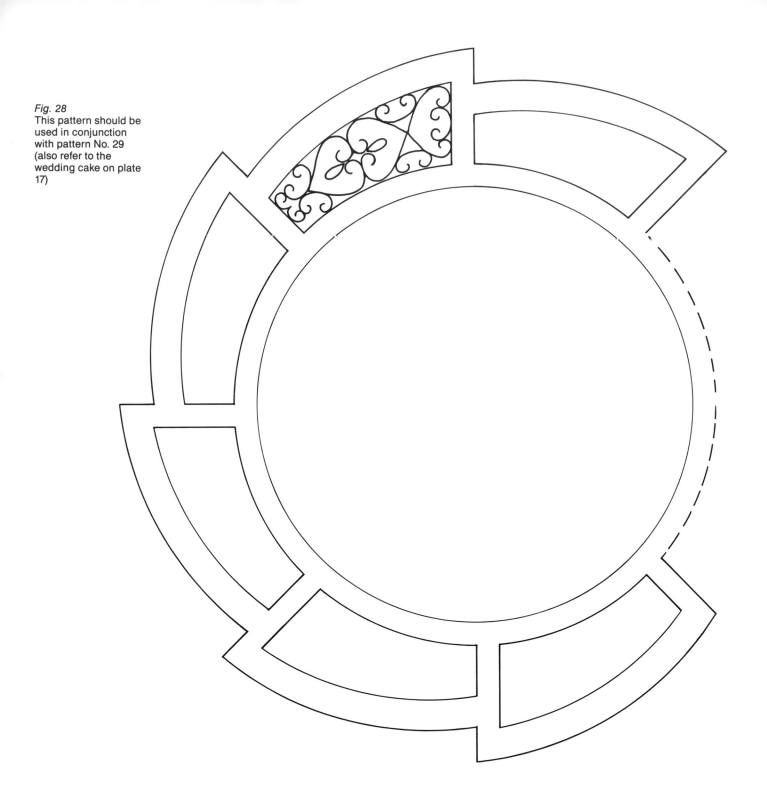

Fig. 28
This pattern should be
used in conjunction
with pattern No. 29
(also refer to the
wedding cake on plate
17)

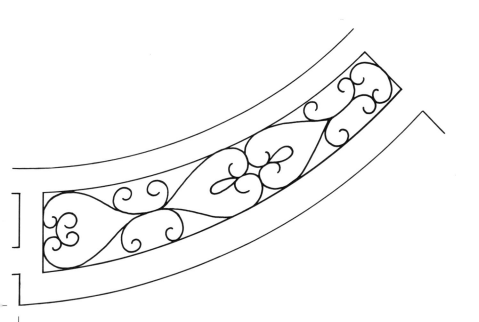

Fig. 29
As can be seen on
plate 17 this collar fits
around the cake at the
bottom

Fig. 30

Fig. 31

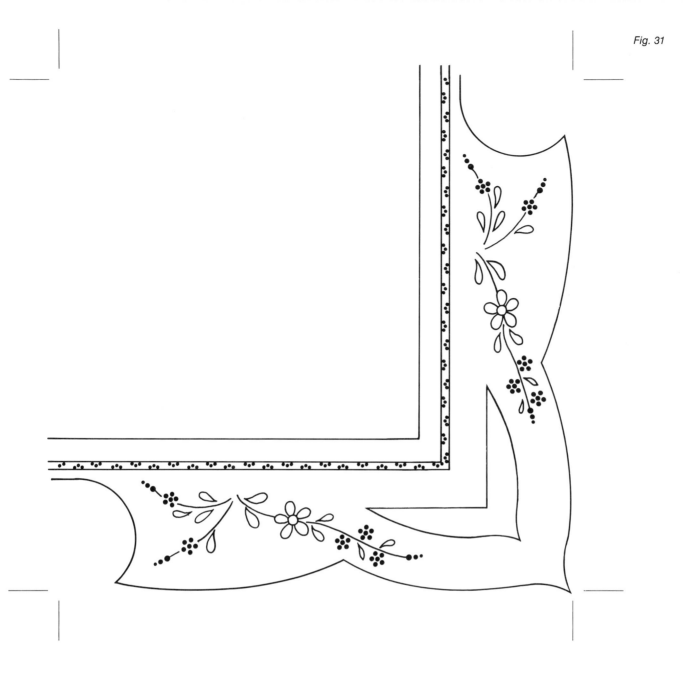

Flood-work and rice-paper patterns

Fig. 32

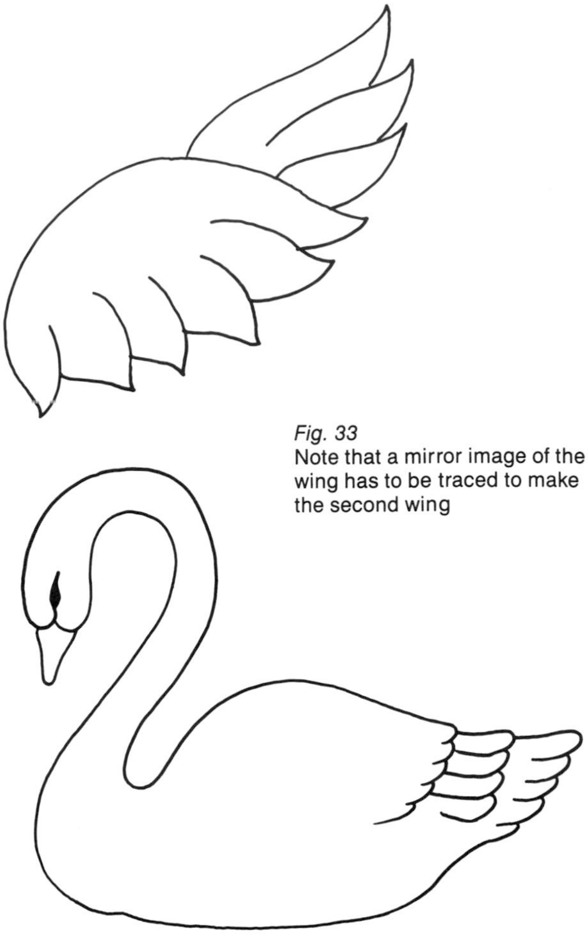

Fig. 33
Note that a mirror image of the wing has to be traced to make the second wing

Fig. 34

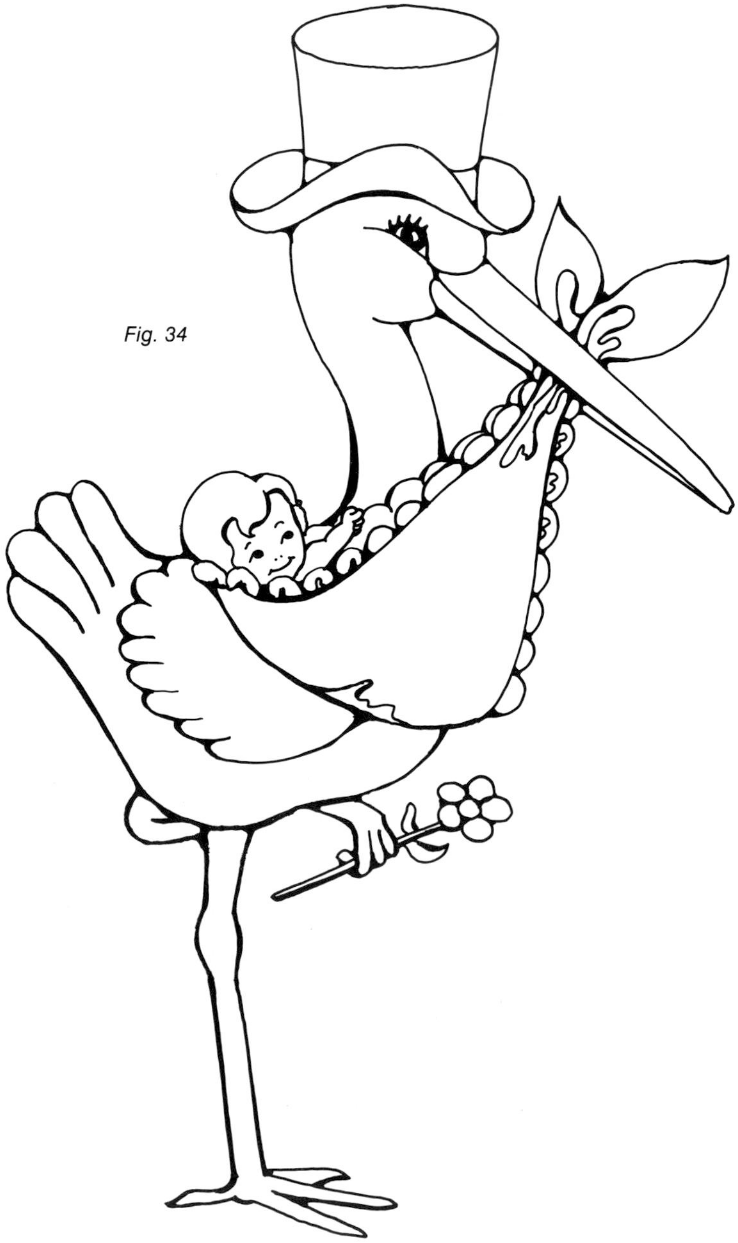

Fig. 35

Fig. 36

Fig. 37

83

Fig. 38

Fig. 39

Fig. 40

Fig. 41

Fig. 42

Fig. 43

Fig. 44

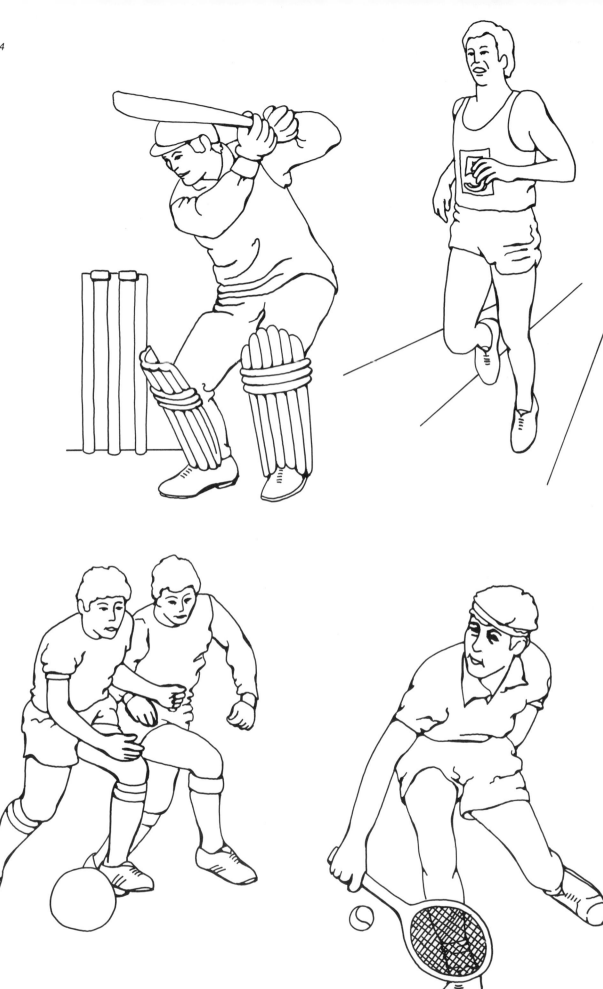

A B C D E
F G H I J
K L M N O P
Q R S T U
V W X Y Z
1 2 3 4 5
6 7 8 9 0

A B C D E
F G H I J
K L M N O P
Q R S T U
V W X Y Z
1 2 3 4 5
6 7 8 9 0

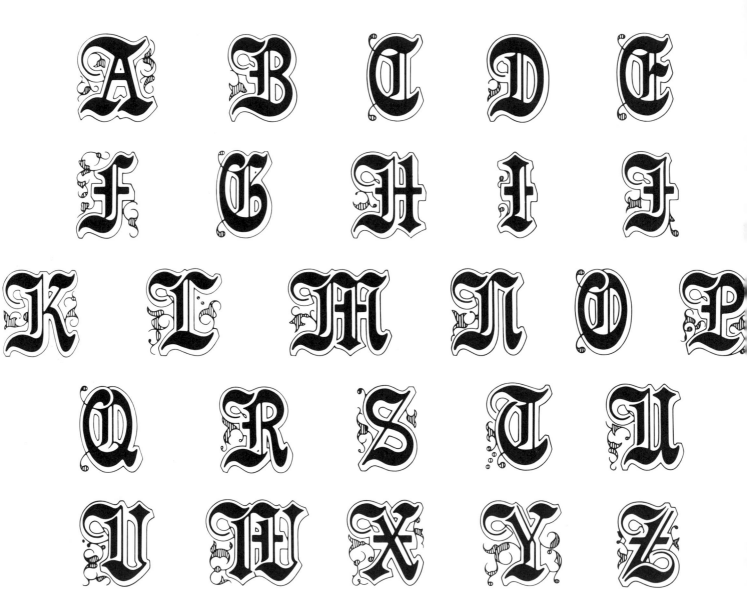

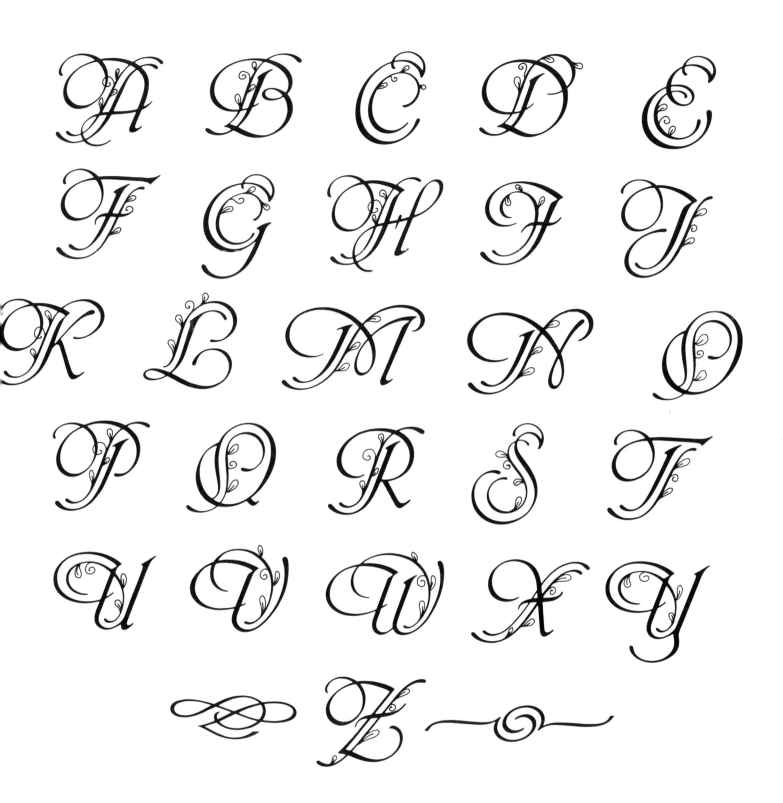

Acknowledgements

People experienced in sugar art will know that cake decorating can be compared with building a house. A building constructor may have a beautiful plan, but he cannot succeed without the help of artisans and masons in order to meet his completion deadline.

My time for writing this book was also limited, but thanks to Louise Steven-Jennings, Cynthia Fletcher, Agata Pomario, Irene Pienaar, Jackie Duncan, Ina Goulden, Aletta la Grange and Gertie du Toit, who all helped with making delicate flowers for the cakes depicted on p. 34 to 68, I was able to meet my deadline.

Louise Steven-Jennings also deserves special mention for helping with the embroidery work. And the credit given to Cynthia Fletcher below appropriate photographs is more than a token of gratitude – her work and the captions are self-evident.

Last but not least, there are three very special people who set beacons on my path to becoming a skilled cake decorator: Kotie van der Spuy my tutor, Retha Mordt whose work I always admired and who always encouraged me, and Eunice Borchers my friend and colleague whose prompting resulted in my writing this book.

KATE VENTER
Spring 1984